NEWSPAPER
JOURNALISM

A PRACTICAL INTRODUCTION

SUSAN PAPE & SUE FEATHERSTONE

SAGE Publications

London ● Thousand Oaks ● New Delhi

SAGE Publications Ltd
1 Oliver's Yard
55 City Road
London EC1Y 1SP

SAGE Publications Inc.
2455 Teller Road
Thousand Oaks, California 91320

SAGE Publications India Pvt Ltd
B-42, Panchsheel Enclave
Post Box 4109
New Delhi 110 017

British Library Cataloguing in Publication data

A catalogue record for this book is available
from the British Library

ISBN 0 7619 4328 5
ISBN 0 7619 4329 3 (pbk)

Library of Congress Control Number: 2004099481

Typeset by C&M Digitals (P) Ltd, Chennai, India
Printed and bound in Great Britain by Athenaeum Press, Gateshead

CONTENTS

ACKNOWLEDGEMENTS

Thanks to all those journalists, media specialists, academics and others who contributed in one way or another to the writing of this book – and that includes both past and present colleagues in various newsrooms and academic institutions.

There are too many people to thank them all individually, however, special thanks must go to Janice Barker, Sarah Carey, Dave Crossland, Tony Harcup, Mike Hutchinson, Marina Lewycka, Nigel Johnson, Dick Taylor and Adam Wolstenholme.

And we must mention: Mark Bradley, Madeleine Brindley, Debbie Davies, Anna Davis, Brian Dennis, Paul Durrant, Jon Grubb, Debbie Hall, James Higgins, Mike Hill, Mo Kazi, Shahid Naqvi, Stuart Minting, Mark Naylor, Chris Page, Lisa Parry, Michael Peel, Jonathan Reed, Peter O'Reilly, Carole Richardson, Vic Robbie, Bruce Smith, Holly Smith, Paul Stimpson, David Todd, David Ward, Joe Watson and Garry Willey. All of you were incredibly patient, answering our questions and giving us information, feedback and advice.

We are also grateful to our students and trainees at Sheffield Hallam University and at Trinity and All Saints College, Leeds, who acted as guinea pigs and sounding boards for some of the material in this book.

We must also thank Julia Hall, Jamilah Ahmed, Rachel Burrows and the rest of the team at Sage for their patience and help.

Thanks to Meg and Annie for their understanding; and to Dandy and Barbara for listening.

Finally, extra special thanks must go to our husbands, Geoff and Kevin, for all their encouragement and support.

Thanks everyone.

OPENING THE NEWSROOM DOOR

There is a popular view that journalists are persons with the words 'scoop' and 'probe' deeply scarred on their hearts. It is assumed that they are professionally dedicated to making public every kind of scandal, infidelity and corruption, both of private persons and official organisations.

K. Williams, *The English Newspaper* (1977: 7)

This chapter:

- introduces the new journalist to the regional and local newspaper office
- explains the roles and responsibilities of the different people working in the newsroom
- considers the structure and layout of a typical newsroom
- explains the skills a new journalist will need to learn and develop.

Opening the newsroom door for the first time is a daunting experience. Phones are ringing, people are rushing about or sitting, heads down, concentrating on the words on a PC screen, tapping away on keyboards or talking on the phone. There's someone over by the coffee machine and there's someone else rifling through a stack of newspapers. Two people are staring earnestly at a picture on a screen. Who are they all and what do they do?

THE INDUSTRY

Before we meet the personalities, it is worth saying a little bit about the industry in which they work.

According to the Newspaper Society – the organisation that represents regional and local newspapers in the UK – 85 per cent of all adults (that is more than 40 million people) regularly read a regional or local newspaper. As the most widely read medium in the country, the regional and local sector outstrips both magazines and the national press.

The regional and local mainstream press can be divided into newspapers that are paid for and those that are distributed or given away free (sometimes known as free sheets). Papers that are paid for include 19 morning and 72 evening dailies, 21 Sundays and over 500 weeklies. In the free sector, there are over 600 weeklies.

There are 119 newspaper groups in Britain, including the smaller independents, but a spate of takeovers in recent years has concentrated ownership to the extent that 20 publishers account for 85 per cent of all regional press titles in the country. The top four are Trinity Mirror (with more than 250 titles), Newsquest, Northcliffe Newspaper Group and Johnston Press.

The regional press employs over 45,000 people – more than a quarter of whom are editorial staff. Here we highlight some of the people you will come across.

THE EDITOR

You may have met the editor already at your interview. Make the most of it because you are unlikely to have many dealings with him or her unless and until you manage to find a major scoop or become a more senior journalist.

The editor hires and fires, has final say over editorial decisions and decides the direction the paper will take on particular issues.

He or she may be a hands-on editor – in which case he or she will spend more time in the newsroom than one who isn't – but managerial and commercial matters take up much of the editor's time and he or she will be involved in seemingly endless meetings dealing with the business end of advertising, circulation, promotion and sales penetration.

A good editor needs diplomacy, according to Vic Robbie, a former editor of the Herald series, which includes the *Farnham Herald*:

> I used to work on the *Daily Mail* where you tend not to have day-to-day contact with your readers, but at Farnham – which was a very community-minded place – you just stepped out of the door and you were collared by somebody. If I saw everyone who wanted to talk to the editor I'd never have got any work done. With a local weekly paper you are very much part of the community and you have to remember you have a responsibility to that community.

DEPUTY EDITOR

The deputy editor will have a larger or smaller role depending on the size of the newspaper. He or she might be responsible for either the editorial and newsroom side of the organisation or, as chief sub-editor, the sub-editing side. The deputy editor might also take responsibility for campaigns, special supplements and promotions.

ASSISTANT EDITOR

On a small, local paper there might be no assistant editor, but, on larger newspapers, there could be as many as two or three, responsible for news and/or features. An assistant editor is also sometimes known as a production editor.

Mike Hill, assistant editor responsible for content at the *Lancashire Evening Post*, says his advice to editorial managers like himself is to keep calm under pressure:

> If you are floundering it has a knock-on effect. Don't get too stressed about things. Someone once said to me, 'The paper's never gone out with an empty front page …' and that's absolutely right. Something will happen or you can take a story from one of the inside pages and turn it into a front-page story. There's always something you can do so don't panic.

NEWS EDITOR

The general news reporter works for the news desk, which is staffed by a news editor and his or her deputies. The number of deputies will depend on the size of the paper. On a large regional daily, for instance, there could be as many as three or four. There might also be a night news editor whose shift will start in the afternoon and finish later that night. On a small weekly free sheet, however, there might be only one person in charge who acts as news editor, chief reporter and feature writer rolled into one.

The news editor is responsible for the flow of copy; assessing the top stories and discussing with the production editor or chief sub which will make a page lead and which could be held over, bumping up copy flow on a quiet day and making a local issue of a national story.

The news editor decides which stories are going to be covered and which reporters are going to cover them. He or she will brief reporters, generally suggesting an angle to take, the length of the story that is required and the deadline for the completed copy. If a news editor asks for a couple of paragraphs on a particular story, a reporter would be wasting time writing 750 words – unless, of course, new and important information comes to light that the news editor had not been aware of, in which case, it is the reporter's job to inform him or her and argue the case for making it longer.

The news editor is the first point of contact when a reporter is out on the road, and he or she will also want to see the copy as it is being written up or, certainly, once it has been written.

Janice Barker, deputy news editor of the *Oldham Evening Chronicle*, says that, apart from a sense of humour and endless patience, news editors need a good nose for a story and excellent time management skills:

> Although it is important for reporters to bring in or spot new stories, the news editor needs to constantly monitor local, regional and national events, making sure stories are not missed and that local angles or implications are brought out. Matching the right reporter to the right job is also a skill. Some reporters handle a funny, light-hearted job better than a hard news story, which needs tenacity and persistence.

It is the news editor's job to 'create' stories on a quiet news day. Barker says that this involves 'raiding' copy from national news agencies, such as the Press Association (PA) or Reuters, getting local opinions about national events, doing vox pops or carrying out a 'top ten' holiday destination survey or something similar.

She believes that news editors are the pivot for the whole newsroom:

> We have to make sure copy is through on time, liaise with photographers, keep subs informed of new stories and stories which fall through or get delayed, track down freelancers and decide which jobs to cover. We have to make sure everything is kept to deadlines because, as soon as one passes, another one has to be met. And there is the administration. News editors are the first people to be asked to answer all the questions other departments in the paper cannot deal with, from missing faxes and e-mails to stories from the past, names, contacts, invoices for freelancers and so on.

Media theorists are much exercised by the role of news editors (and reporters and editors too) in creating news. It is a tricky issue. While journalists maintain that decisions about news are based on the need and expectation of their readers to be kept informed about what is happening in their community, theorists emphasise the artificial nature of these decisions.

Walter Gieber, for instance, in a 1956 American study, suggested that what he called newspaper people were primarily task-orientated, motivated not by 'the evaluative nature of news but [by] the pressures of getting copy into the newspaper' (Gieber in Tumber 1999: 219).

Certainly, Mike Hill's earlier comment that an empty front page can be filled with a story from the nether regions of the paper implies that a certain arbitrary quality attaches to the notion of newsworthiness. This certainly gives the suggestion that news values are not absolute but relative. Indeed, Chris Page, editor of the *Selby Times*, admits that news values change at different times of the year:

> There will be times during silly seasons – quiet periods, perhaps, when news sources are on holiday – when we may have to dig deeper for hard news and take a more feature style and in-depth approach.

In this context, news, as Gieber suggests, is indeed what 'newspapermen make it' (Gieber in Tumber 1999: 18).

Further, a good news editor must be able to spot talent in a reporter, says Paul Durrant, assistant editor of the *Eastern Daily Press*:

> We might have a relatively raw junior who hasn't learned everything about hard news yet but might know something about a certain subject. I am a great believer in horses for courses. I always ask reporters what they know about more than anything else – they might not have learned all the tricks of the trade in hard news terms, but they might know a lot about something else that could come in useful; they still have something to bring to the party.

SUB-EDITORS

'Subs', as they are known, work under the chief sub-editor and edit the paper. On larger newspapers there will be subs responsible for specific pages, such as news, features or sport, but on smaller papers, a sub would be expected to work on every page. While their job includes designing pages and laying out stories, adding headlines, bylines, standfirsts (text under a headline with extra information, often including a byline) and picture captions, one of their most important responsibilities involves checking a reporter's copy once the news editor, features editor or sports editor has seen it. They check for accuracy and will correct spelling mistakes and any other grammatical errors. Subs also check copy for potential libel and contempt. That is not to say a reporter can hand in sloppy work thinking that the sub will automatically correct it for them. As a reporter, you must read and check your own work, make sure spellings are correct, ensure that the copy is grammatical and that it reads clearly and well and that it is written in line with the newspaper's own house style.

The sub will ask a reporter to rewrite a story or certainly rejig it if there are too many problems with it. One colleague remembers that at a local newspaper where she was a trainee reporter, the subs would pin on the wall examples of poor writing and sloppy copy: total humiliation for the writer. It is better for a reporter to cultivate a good working relationship with the subs. Rather than treating them as the enemy who are going to pull a story to pieces, think of them as another pair of eyes on a story.

Debbie Hall, assistant publications editor for Hull Daily Mail Publications, says a keen trainee can learn a lot from comparing their original copy with the version that finally appears in the paper:

One of the worst things reporters do is not get to the point quickly enough. It means I've got to trawl through the whole thing and rewrite it to get the main points in the intro. Careless spelling and punctuation are also common failings, they're particular bugbears of mine, especially when people see how their copy has been changed but still keep making the same mistakes – for instance, double spacing after every full point. I remember one reporter who did that. It meant whoever subbed her work had to be continually closing it up. Spellings are the other big problem area. You should always get people's names right and the names of streets, too. There's a Leads Road in Hull that regularly gets written as Leeds Road.

It's the avoidable mistakes that really grate, like changing people's names in copy. I've seen stories where Mr Jackson becomes Mr Johnson halfway through. It's a daft mistake to make and, if it's at the end of a long shift, it's possible a sub might miss it. Alternatively, the reporter might have gone home or gone out on another job so I or another sub have got to try and track down their contact, which might take two or three phone calls and, if you're waiting to finish off a page, it can become unnecessarily time-consuming, not to mention annoying.

AND THE OTHERS ...

The newsroom will also include a chief reporter, general reporters who work from the main newsroom and, in some cases, district reporters, who either travel out to cover a particular geographical patch within the newspaper's circulation area or operate from sub-offices or from home. In one sense, theirs is a harder job than that of a head office-based reporter as they work largely off-diary and are expected to find their own stories relevant to the patch that they are covering.

The pace of newsroom life means there is little time for 'nannying' new recruits. Rookies are expected to stand on their own two feet almost from day one and, although most of today's junior reporters will complete a National Council for the Training of Journalists (NCTJ) accredited course before securing their first job, the real learning starts in the newsroom – as Mo Kazi, an NCTJ student, discovered during a work experience stint on the *Derby Evening Telegraph*:

> I was a little nervous. So many people and computers. One of the first things I did was a vox pop and I have to admit that it was scary approaching people, especially when they didn't want to cooperate, but I knew I just had to carry on until I got the six quotes that the news editor wanted. Once I got into the groove of things it was not too bad, although, after I had interviewed the first three people, I realised I had forgotten to ask for their addresses, so I had to start all over again. I certainly learnt from that mistake. It was valuable experience. It made me realise that if I'm to make it, I just have to get on with it and forget about being shy.

A good reporter, says Chris Page, editor of the *Selby Times*, is someone who can combine the roles of gathering and writing news:

> Some are good at research and interview. Others are good at articulating that information in print, quickly and clearly. Few, initially at least, are good at both. As an editor I want someone who not only exhibits these qualities but someone who is, first and foremost, a people person – someone who can elicit with equal ease information from shop floor to boardroom. Those self-same communication skills also make the best newsroom team player.

THE SPECIALISTS

The newsrooms of large regional dailies will include a number of specialist reporters whose job it is to concentrate on one particular specialism, such as health, crime, education or sport (sport reporters generally occupy their own area and are overseen by a sports editor).

Then there are feature writers, who write features, background articles, profiles and reviews. The features area might include lifestyle page writers, covering fashion, food and lifestyle.

However, none of this is to say that a general news reporter will not be required at some time to write a feature, a sports story or a review.

The picture desk generally includes a picture editor and a team of photographers. Reporters and photographers are expected to liaise on stories – how else will a photographer know what sort of picture to take to accompany your story if he or she has not spoken to you? And there is nothing to stop a reporter from developing an eye for a good picture and making a suggestion to the photographer.

On many stories, a reporter and photographer will work together – something one colleague feels ambivalent about: 'On the one hand they can be company if you are having to hang about for an interviewee, and they can give you confidence if the story you are working on is in a slightly dodgy area, but, on the other, it can be incredibly frustrating waiting for a photographer to take "just one more" picture of the person you are waiting to interview because "just one more picture" means at least a dozen.'

Worse, though, says another colleague, are the 'helpful' photographers, who keep butting in during the interview, asking irrelevant and distracting questions:

> They keep going off at a tangent and it's really difficult to follow the threads of the interview because they've asked all sorts of irrelevant things. I don't mind a photographer chipping in now and again – it makes the interview feel more like a conversation and helps the interviewee relax – but it drives me mad if they forget I'm supposed to be in the driving seat.

There is, to put it bluntly, no easy way of shutting them up either. Most regional newspaper photographers have been working their patch far longer than their usually much younger reporting counterparts. They are often a valuable source of tip-offs and contacts and suggesting that they 'butt out' is likely to be counter-productive in the long run. Instead, if you find the photographer leading the interviewee into an unproductive area of questioning, make a (written) note of the next question you want to ask (it will act as a memory prompt) and wait patiently for a natural break in the conversation.

AGENCIES AND FREELANCERS

Freelance journalists supply stories to local, regional and national newspapers and the PA. You will find that many of them go through local and regional newspapers picking out good stories to sell on to the nationals.

A freelancer could be someone working on their own or as part of an agency, which can be anything from a two-man business to national organisations, such as the PA and Reuters.

NEWSROOM DIARY

The newsroom diary is one of the most vital tools in the office. Details will be logged in here of forthcoming events – from a local flower show to court cases – and anniversaries – for instance, the first 12 months in office of the new council or the anniversary of a notorious local murder.

Alongside each entry will be the initials of which reporter is to cover it. It is essential to check the diary on arrival in the office and it is worth checking it at frequent intervals during the day as it will be continually updated by news desk staff.

The news editor or a member of the news desk enters dates in the diary from information they have received from press releases, calls and tip-offs.

DEADLINES

Journalists are ruled by deadlines. Miss one and your story will not make it into the paper.

All newspapers have deadlines – for written copy, finished pages, printing, hitting the streets – but different newspapers have different deadlines. For instance, a local weekly paper, such as the *Farnham Herald*, which is on the streets by Thursday lunchtime (although it carries a Friday dateline), has a final copy deadline as late as between 5 and 6 pm on a Wednesday. Pages are tied up by between 6 and 7 pm and the paper is printed first thing the following day. This does not mean to say that reporters can relax until Wednesday and then have a mad burst of story writing. Instead, they spread the workload, writing earlier in the week for less time-sensitive pages, such as features and sport.

A regional evening newspaper has tighter deadlines throughout each day because first editions are out on the streets by mid-morning. At the *Lancashire Evening Post*, for instance, the first edition hits the stands at 11.30 am, so reporters writing for the early edition have a copy deadline of 9.30 am. For the two later editions, copy deadlines are 10.30 am and 11.30 am. On a regional evening newspaper, some pages, such as features, will have been worked on the previous day or overnight, but the front page, main news pages and some sports pages will need to be filled on the day.

A regional daily might have less concentration on absolute deadlines and more on page scheduling. At the *Eastern Daily Press*, the back dozen pages must be finished by lunchtime or just after, so Paul Durrant will tell his reporters to have stories finished by then. Deadlines for stories for the front end of the newspaper are between 5 and 7 pm, while breaking stories will be expected between 9 and 11 pm.

The first edition (of five) of the *Eastern Daily Press* goes at 10.40 pm and the final edition at 1.45 am – although this is a movable feast depending on the quality of any late-breaking story and the size of the paper.

CONFERENCES

Every newspaper will have news conferences and these will be greater or smaller events depending on the type and size of the newspaper and the number of journalists attending the meeting. At the weekly *Farnham Herald*, former editor Vic Robbie held a news conference as soon as the current paper had gone off to the printers on a Thursday to discuss the following week's paper with the chief reporter and some staff reporters. He held another news conference the following Monday to see how stories were developing and a further conference on the Wednesday morning to check that everything was going to plan and to consider late bids for the main news pages.

By contrast, a regional daily will have more than one conference each day. The first one will be at around 10 am and might include just the news editor, sports editor, features editor, business and picture editor. A later conference, at between 2 and 3 pm, will be more formal and include the editor, departmental heads and the sports desk. A further conference will be held between 5 and 6 pm, with the same people checking that what was said at the earlier afternoon conference was still current. This conference is more of a confirmation and handover to the night news editor and the night editor, but will include discussion on what is going on the front page and what the main headlines are.

One of the first things editor Terry Manners did on joining the *Western Daily Press* was to bring forward all deadlines. Former associate editor Peter O'Reilly (now editor of the *Bristol Observer*) says that the old concept of 'news' is now almost dead in the water as TV, radio and the Internet are breaking news stories every minute of the day: 'So holding the whole newspaper back for breaking news is an anachronism because it is almost 12 hours later when you come out on the street.'

The *Western Daily Press* news desk starts at 7 am and the first deadline is to have all the various news lists in time for the first conference at 11 am. By 12.15 pm, the first stories are going to page. As O'Reilly says:

> From then on it is a case of ensuring a smooth flow of copy for subs who build up the pages during the afternoon. The main deadline of the day is 6 pm by which time the editor has designed Page 1 and the final shape of the newspaper is known. The day news desk then hands over to the night news desk and the new team takes the paper through until midnight, during which period any changes can be made based on our four editions going at various times. Copy deadline from the newsdesk to subs for the first edition is 9.30 pm and then each half hour through to the City Final.

CALLS

'Doing the calls' is an important task for any reporter. It means calling all the local emergency services to check if anything is happening. With fast, digital telephone dialling and, in many cases, automated pre-recorded messages at the other end, it is a straightforward job, although it should be stressed that most good reporters would prefer to speak to the police direct than listen to a voice bank.

If you call the police phone line and pick up a pre-recorded message about a particular incident, but there is not enough information given, you must call the police press office for further details.

Thankfully there are still areas where newspaper reporters will contact the local police, fire and ambulance stations personally – either by phone or in person.

Whichever method is used, a reporter 'doing the calls' should make a friend of the services they contact and listen carefully to what is said. Odd throwaway lines often produce good stories, too.

SHIFTS

If you want to work 9 to 5, then perhaps being a journalist is not for you. Working on a newspaper involves working shifts and long, odd and late hours.

As first editions of regional evening newspapers hit the news-stands by mid-morning, reporters must start work between 7 and 8 am, working until somewhere between 3.30 and 4.30 pm.

The majority of staff on a regional daily will work from about 10 am to between 6 and 7 pm, but an early reporter might be expected to start work at 8.30 am, and late reporters at 2 pm and perhaps 6 pm, working later into the evening and night.

In addition, don't forget, that many of the meetings and events a reporter is expected to cover are held in the evenings and at weekends, such as council meetings, community, sports and arts events. A colleague recalls the many times she has arrived home after a day's work and settled down with a meal, only to find the phone ringing with an urgent request from the news desk to chase a late-breaking story.

For Mark Bradley, editor at the *Wakefield Express*, the unpredictable nature of the newsroom day is part of its charm: 'I think that's one of the best things about being a journalist – having the freedom to learn and experience new things and the opportunity to create something readers want to read.'

David Todd, assistant editor at the *Sheffield Star*, agrees. 'In some ways it is a very unstructured sort of job. There's a lot of variety and you're not stuck in a 9 to 5 routine.'

USING THE CUTTINGS SERVICE

Most newsrooms now store back copies of newspapers and stories electronically and they can be accessed by journalists from their PCs. (Cuttings got their name from the fact that they were literally that: stories cut from newspapers, filed in envelopes under appropriate reference headings.)

Today's digital system is generally operated by a librarian or IT specialist. Although few modern newsrooms now have a library as such, there should be dictionaries and reference books available such as *Who's Who* and *Crockford's Clerical Directory*, encyclopaedias and atlases.

A word of warning, though: although the database is an important source of information, journalists need to be aware of the importance of evaluating physical sources as carefully as they would human ones. This particularly applies to cuttings from other publications. As Lynette Sheridan Burns (2000: 96) observes: 'A journalist conducting an interview is always aware that a news source may be actively manipulating the information presented. However, a journalist using another journalist's published work may be accepting at face value that the first journalist got it right.'

It is important to apply the same rigorous critical criteria to every source of information. In the case of a cutting, for instance, has the original writer got the facts right? For whom are they writing and what is the purpose of the piece – entertainment, education or information? The answers to both these questions will affect the tone and slant as well as the selection of information. Put simply, you do not know what the original writer has excluded that might be pertinent to your purposes.

Be particularly sceptical about the Internet as a source of information. Yes, it is a useful tool and can provide valuable background information, but, again, reporters need to ask who posted this information and why? Remember, the Internet is largely unregulated and almost anyone can post almost anything they like, which means it can be difficult to verify essential facts.

AND ELSEWHERE ...

Elsewhere within the newspaper building you will find advertising sales staff, responsible for display and classified ads. Many reporters will quietly – and reluctantly – admit that a newspaper would struggle without the revenue generated by advertising, but it does not make it any easier when stories are cut because a quarter page ad has been placed at the last minute. However, it does not do any harm to keep in contact with the advertising department and certainly to check the small ads in the newspaper when it comes out as many a story has been buried in the 'for sale' and 'wanted' sections. Checking the births, deaths and marriages section for possible stories is essential, too.

Promotions and marketing are departments a reporter will come into contact with now and then, especially when competitions are being run in the newspaper and it is the reporter's job to interview the winner.

Don't forget the front counter staff. These are the people in the front line when members of the public – often those all-important readers – visit the newspaper to place an ad, pay a bill or speak to a reporter.

Exercise

Having read this chapter, make a list of what you consider to be the essential qualities for a good journalist.

(Answers are given at the end of the book.)

WHAT IS NEWS?

News is what a chap who doesn't care much about anything wants to read. And it's only news until he's read it. After that it's dead.

E. Waugh, *Scoop* (1982)

This chapter:

- examines the definitions of news
- asks what makes something newsworthy
- looks at different types of news stories
- questions who decides what is newsworthy
- looks at how journalists identify stories.

Various attempts have been made to answer the question 'What is news?' It is a tricky one. Lynette Sheridan Burns (2000: 50), for instance, in *Understanding Journalism* defines news as something that binds 'people together in a sense of community'. Certainly, freelance journalist Carole Richardson buys into the notion of community – at least in the sense that news is something that individuals want to share with one another. 'News is something you *have* to tell a friend before the credits on your mobile phone run out,' she says – a definition that suggests an element of urgency, which is an element that is somewhat lacking from the universally accepted assertion, usually credited to former editor of *The Sunday Times*, Harold Evans, that news is people.

On one level, it is hard to argue with any of these descriptions, yet none of them tells the whole story. Indeed, although most journalists would reach some sort of consensus on what constitutes the key ingredients of news, it is unlikely that they would agree on a precise definition. Some would say that it is something new that has just happened or is about to happen; something that is immediate, exciting, unusual, unexpected, amazing, vital, important and interesting.

Others would describe it as newly received, fresh information that has not been published or broadcast before. Adam Wolstenholme, a reporter on the *Dewsbury Reporter*, adds a further qualification: 'News should be something surprising, something we didn't already know, that will either affect the readers directly or, as in the case of a "human interest" story, inspire their empathy or interest.'

Another colleague defines news as something that could pass the 'pub door test' – that is, if you burst into a pub with some information and managed to get everyone to stop what they were doing and listen to you, you would have a decent story on your hands. Alan Powell, editor of the *Sheffield Telegraph*, puts it even more succinctly: 'News is what you talk about over a pint.'

This is all very well for national reporting, but, as Adam Wolstenholme observes:

> Local journalists will write plenty of stories that are of enormous interest to their readers, but would mean nothing to someone "down the pub" in the next city. Essentially banal subject matter, like roadworks, for instance, can be a great source of local stories because they have a genuine impact on people's day-to-day lives. You have to bear in mind, therefore, not just what excites you as an individual, but what will excite your readers, who might live in a different town and have very different interests.

LOCATION, LOCATION, LOCATION ...

Adam Wolstenholme's observation is interesting on a number of counts. First, because it introduces the idea of location – that news is only news if it happens in the right place. So, the *Selby Times* devoted pages of coverage to the Selby train crash, which occurred on the very limits of its geographical circulation area, while the neighbouring *Pontefract and Castleford Express*, the circulation boundaries of which fall just metres short of the crash site, had less to say about the crash and instead concentrated on the efforts of the medical teams at Pontefract Hospital to treat the injured. Other regionals would have checked the list of victims to see if any came from their circulation area. They would have given the story more or less coverage depending on whether or not there was a strong local angle.

Second, Wolstenholme makes it clear that news does not necessarily have to be either dramatic or exciting. The most mundane occurrence – roadworks, say – may be newsworthy simply because of the scale of the impact that it has on the lives of ordinary people. Diversions and long tailbacks for rush hour motorists may not be hugely important in the great scale of things – unless, of course, you happen to be a tired and hungry driver stuck at the back of the queue, in which case, they become immensely significant. That brings us to the third point – news is not just about people, it *affects* people. News impacts on their lives, even if, in the case of the rush hour motorists, it means something as simple as changing their route to avoid traffic hold-ups.

Finally, although he does not say so directly, Wolstenholme implies that news must be based on facts, not fiction. This emphasis is significant. 'Facts,' the late Paul Foot is quoted as saying, in *The Penguin Book of Journalism: Secrets of the press* (Glover 2000: 80), 'are the crucial standard by which opinion can be judged'. Without facts, it becomes impossible for individuals to make accurate, informed judgements about the community in which they live. This is important – locally, nationally and globally. Essentially, journalism acts as 'our means of contact with a world which, though shrinking, is still largely beyond our direct, personal experience. It provides the information from which we draw our "cognitive maps" of reality' (McNair 2001: 21).

Our acceptance of the truthfulness and accuracy of the word pictures that journalists, or rather, reporters, paint when they describe what is happening at home and elsewhere informs our opinions about events and issues outside our own narrow compass, thus, underlining the role that journalism plays in maintaining and reinforcing democracy. Ian Hargreaves (2003: 25), former editor of *The Independent* newspaper and *New Statesman* magazine, and a former professor of journalism at Cardiff University, but now group director of corporate and public affairs at BAA, believes that this is why, above all else, reporting the news matters. 'Good journalism provides the information and opinion upon which successful democratic societies depend. Corrupt that and you corrupt everything.' Without such knowledge and understanding, it would be all too easy for those in power and authority to pull the wool over our eyes.

During the 2003 Iraq war, Mohammed Saeed al-Sahaf, the Ba'ath party's minister for information, was roundly ridiculed for what one journalist described as his promotion of the party line – assuring the world that all was well, even as battles raged visibly behind him ('Free to do bad things', *The Guardian*, 12 April 2003). Iraq's authorities recognised only too well the importance of spinning a good war and controlling the images and information conveyed through the media, both to their own domestic audience and the wider global community.

By the same token, both British and American governments were highly critical of what they termed the pro-Iraq bias of some UK and US media coverage. A spokesman for Prime Minister Tony Blair accused the BBC – in particular, its Baghdad-based correspondents Rageh Omaar and Andrew Gilligan – of 'trying to make the news rather than reporting it' ('Free to do bad things', *The Guardian*, 12 April 2003).

Gilligan (now better known for the events that led up to the Hutton Inquiry), who was targeted after he reported that people of Baghdad were experiencing their 'first days of freedom in more fear than they had ever known before' ('Rageh Omaar wins it for BBC in Baghdad', *The Guardian*, 14 April 2003), was defended by his Today colleague John Humphrys, who said: 'We are not part of the propaganda war. We are meant to do what, in my view, Andrew Gilligan has done brilliantly over the past few weeks, which is telling us what he sees and hears.' ('BBC defends its reporter in Baghdad', *The Observer*, 13 April 2003)

In a sense, the fact that the press were being squeezed from both sides suggests that they were on the right track in terms of presenting the facts truthfully and impartially. This is a journalistic truism that applies at both local and national levels. As Adam Wolstenholme says: 'There are times when one feels exasperated by people who want only their point of view to be publicised, but then annoying people is something we inevitably have to do from time to time. Once, when I complained to my former news editor at the *Spenborough Guardian*, Margaret Heward, that I was being berated by people on both sides of a squabble that I'd done a story on, she told me that it probably meant that I'd done a good job and it's when you take flak from only one side that you might have messed up.

NEWS IS ABOUT FINDING OUT WHAT'S GOING ON

In part, this is what makes journalism such a rewarding profession – in reporting what is important and newsworthy, journalists have an opportunity to draw to public attention matters that might otherwise be ignored. 'The business of the press,' said nineteenth-century editor of *The Times*, Thaddeus Delane, 'is disclosure' (Delane in Wheen 2002: xi). For Wolstenholme, this notion of finding things out goes to the heart of the news business:

I like to be in search of the truth. Reporters who feel envious of the money people make in PR should console themselves with the thought that reporters, unlike PR people, are basically after the unbiased truth, rather than spinning a line. In spite of the bad press we sometimes get, I think we are essentially doing something worthwhile.

The role of *The Sunday Times* in securing compensation for the thalidomide babies and that of Bernstein and Woodward in exposing the complicity of

President Nixon in the Watergate break-in are prime examples of this kind of pure journalism – newsmaking that is driven by what Philip Knightley, who spent five years on the thalidomide investigation, describes as 'moral indignation, outrage at the sheer efforts of men who could put pecuniary interests before their victims' lives' (Knightley in de Burgh 2001: 22).

WHOSE TRUTH IS IT ANYWAY?

It is easy at this point to become almost evangelical about the role of journalists. However, an implicit trust in the truthfulness of journalism argues a lack of understanding about the nature of truth as the way in which facts are presented can persuade readers to 'see' the news in a particular way. At a very simple level, journalists select and interpret 'news' so that it fits and influences the culture of understanding of its readership. The aim is to achieve a 'balance between satisfying reader demands and shaping the news to influence what the readership understands' (Lacey and Longman 1997: 194–5).

Journalists may strive for objectivity, but, rightly or wrongly, their perceptions about news are determined primarily by what, in their view, their readers will consider newsworthy. This is a complicated and, for theorists, a somewhat problematical issue, but, broadly speaking, as Marina Lewykca, a senior lecturer at Sheffield Hallam University, observes, journalists tend to see themselves as contributing to an informed democracy, while theorists see their role as creating consensus and confirming ideology.

The upshot of all this ambiguity about the nature of news, however, is that a trawl through one day's newspapers will produce a wide variety of different stories on different subjects, none of which appear to be linked in any way, yet each one is defined as news. Hence, front page news in *The Sun* was 'Never a rape: snooker case insult to real victims', which is not necessarily front page news in *The Daily Telegraph*, which has instead 'Tear up chaotic planning reforms, say MPs', nor is it front page news in the *Daily Mail*, which has 'Who cares? At 108, Alice Knight starved herself to death, a despairing victim of how our old people's homes have been wrecked by red tape and cost-cutting'. Each choice reflects the perceptions and priorities of the readers of each publication – or the editors' perceptions of what these are – demonstrating both the symbiotic relationship between journalist and reader and the truism that there can be no single classification that sums up news in a nutshell.

Chris Page, editor of the *Selby Times*, sees his paper as an integral part of the local community, campaigning and crusading on local issues as well as offering an informative package of exclusive news, features and photos, sport and grass roots stuff, such as what's on and leisure information, as well as letters, competitions and promotions:

It's important to get the mix right. On a local newspaper like ours, people are quick to pick up the telephone and tell you if they're not happy about something. By the same token, they will also let you know when they like what they're reading. Such feedback is invaluable. It means we're able to respond to our readers and to be sensitive about what they expect from us. The important thing, though, is that we should always be telling readers something new, something they didn't know before, about people or events in their community.

YES, BUT IS IT NEWS?

What is a journalist looking for when he or she sets off on a news story? What is it that makes one person more newsworthy than another? Why is a news journalist likely to consider covering one event but not another?

The answers to all these questions depend on a number of factors. Timing, for instance, is hugely important. Former government spin doctor Jo Moore became infamous for her advice that September 11 would be a good day to bury bad news. What she meant was that stories that might otherwise be front page fodder would be ignored by journalists and readers alike under the weight of news generated by the New York and Washington terrorist attacks. Similarly, stories that might be ignored on a busy news day achieve a disproportionate importance at quiet times of year – the August silly season, which regularly spawns a raft of stories about the Loch Ness Monster and other improbable happenings, is a classic example.

The celebrity (or notoriety) of the person concerned also matters. Nobody really cares if student Wills A. N. Other marches through the streets clutching a Tesco carrier bag. However, as soon as Prince William does the same, it is a safe bet that his picture will be splashed across the tabloids. Significantly, the newsworthiness of the story is reinforced by the possession of a good, clear photograph as 'pictures govern things to an extent', Adam Wolstenholme admits.

The picture, in fact, adds impetus to a weak story – after all, Prince William, poor lad, has to buy his groceries somewhere.

By the same token, an appealing photograph can add weight to a story that, by any standards, might be deemed newsworthy. 'Sadly, a missing teenager has more chance of making the front page if there's a good-quality picture of her looking sweet and pretty,' says Wolstenholme.

Such stories also possess the vitally important news qualities of drama and rarity. Because murder and rape remain, mercifully, uncommon, they are, therefore, correspondingly bigger news than events that occur more frequently. They are dramatic and immediate and, from the point of view of the reader, do not require detailed explanation or interpretation – they are easy to understand and absorb. Murder equals a victim equals tragedy – stories do not come much more straightforward than that. Economic, social and cultural trends, on the other hand, take place over a much longer period of time – they, by and large, unfold rather than explode into our cultural consciousness and, because of their complexity, lack the immediacy and drama usually associated with news. The only exceptions to this rule concern the release of statistical reports or surveys – for instance, a study into the link between adult violence and the viewing habits of children – or a special inquiry, for example, into the death of a child in the care of social workers.

Former broadsheet newspaper editor Ian Jack, currently editor of *Granta* magazine, puts this preoccupation with the dramatic and the immediate down to the fact that '... Britain has developed a singular sort of media culture which places a high premium on excitement, controversy and sentimentality, in which information takes second place to the opinions it arouses' (Jack in Wheen 2002: xiii).

On one level, his comment could be read as suggesting that modern journalism is shallow and sensationalist. Some of it perhaps is. However, another interpretation might be that journalists seek to write news stories that excite, stimulate and move their readers while also provoking discussion and debate.

Chris Page, editor of the *Selby Times*, finds it hard to define the precise nature of news, saying: 'News is news is news. Journalists develop an innate ability to know what it is – a taste.'

In a sense, he is spot on – journalists do seem to develop a taste for news and most of us never question or interrogate the specific nature of the tastes that we acquire. Theorists, on the other hand, are much exercised by this. It was only when Tony Harcup, a lecturer at the University of Sheffield, moved from freelance journalism to academia that he realised just how much academic time and energy had been spent on trying to understand the journalist's craft.

While initially the names John Galtung and Mari Ruge had meant nothing to him, he soon discovered that the Norwegian academics had produced a classic list of 12 factors that they identified as being particularly pertinent in the selection of news. These were, in order of importance, frequency, threshold, unambiguity, meaningfulness, consonance, unexpectedness, continuity, composition, reference to elite nations, reference to elite people, reference to persons, reference to something negative (Fowler 1991: 13). Harcup, however, thought that this list was fundamentally flawed and that over-dependence on the 40-year-old Norwegian study of foreign news stories was the academic equivalent of the cuttings job. Dissatisfied, he and colleague Deirdre O'Neill carried out a detailed month-long analysis of more than a thousand page lead news stories in three national newspapers and produced a new list that they felt better represented the news values of working UK journalists (Harcup 2004: 36).

Although they acknowledge that there are exceptions to every rule, they conclude that news stories must generally conform to one or more of the following criteria:

- *The power elite*: stories concerning powerful individuals, organisations or institutions.
- *Celebrity*: stories concerning people who are already famous.
- *Entertainment*: stories concerning sex, show business, human interest, animals, an unfolding drama or offering opportunities for humorous treatment, entertaining photographs or witty headlines.
- *Surprise*: stories that have an element of surprise or contrast.
- *Bad news*: stories with particularly negative overtones, such as conflict or tragedy.
- *Good news*: stories with particularly positive overtones, such as rescues or cures.
- *Magnitude*: stories that are perceived as sufficiently significant, either in terms of the number of people involved or their potential impact.
- *Relevance*: stories about issues, groups and nations perceived to be relevant to the audience.
- *Follow-ups*: stories about subjects already in the news.
- *Newspaper's agenda*: stories that set or fit the news organisation's own agenda.

SO, BACK TO THE QUESTION: IS IT NEWS?

At a very simple level, all news stories answer the questions 'Who?' and 'What?' Who has the story happened to? What has happened to them? The best stories will also tell the reader where it happened, why it happened, when it happened and how it happened, but, almost without exception, news stories concern people and what has happened to them.

In addition, news stories may also be split into two distinct categories – hard news and soft news. Hard news stories are those that deal with topical events or issues that have an immediate or catastrophic or life-changing effect on the individuals concerned. In short, hard news is (often) bad news and often deals with serious matters that require equal weight to be attached to both the who and the what. For instance, a terrorist hijacking an aeroplane is hard news. So is a murder or rape.

Soft news, on the other hand, has more of a human interest focus and, although, in the short term at least, events may be equally immediate or important for the individuals concerned, they are rarely life-changing in quite the same way. Accordingly, an exposé in *The Guardian* newspaper on 7 March 2003 about the involvement of a UK company in building a chemical warfare plant in Iraq – 'Dismay at chemical plant link' – is hard news, while a story in the same edition about a survey into the sums paid out by the parental tooth fairy – 'Tooth fairy posts 100% dividend' – is unmistakably soft news. Both have their place within a lively, modern newspaper.

WHAT MAKES A STORY NEWSWORTHY?

As well as the definitions of news that we looked at earlier, a simple guide as to what makes a story newsworthy follows. A story is newsworthy if it is:

- something that affects a lot of people – new legislation, political or social issues, jumbo jet crash, for example
- bad (or hard) news – accidents, such as plane and rail crashes, terrorist attacks and so on
- of human interest – elderly pensioner leaves care home for mansion after winning the Lottery or brave toddler undergoes heart and lung transplant would fall into this category
- topical – contains a 'today' line
- informative – informs the reader of something new
- unexpected – lightning strikes York Minster, fire breaks out at Windsor Castle, death of the Princess of Wales and so on
- something that deals with a subject that is currently in vogue – such as road rage, hospital bugs
- a local or national disgrace – town councillor spotted in brothel, MP in drugs scandal, say
- of general interest – that is, interesting to the widest possible audience
- something that involves celebrity – the Beckhams' private lives, Liam Gallagher's love life, a soap star's collagen lip injections and similar

- geographically appropriate to the receiver – stories from Aberdeen, Derby and Reigate are of less interest to readers in Yorkshire, for instance, than those from Harrogate, Leeds and Wakefield
- dramatic – life-saving rescues, medical breakthroughs and so on feature here
- campaigning – examples here would be save our schools, don't close our cottage hospital
- superlative – man grows tallest sunflower in Britain, I've got the first ever … longest … smallest … and other such stories
- sexy – *Big Brother* housemate caught in secret romp with Page 3 girl, for example
- seasonal – it's nearly Christmas so let's look at the odds of snow or it's Easter, so let's do something about chocolate or it's summer – is there a drought?
- amazing – 110-year-old great-grandfather still swims 20 lengths every day in local pool, woman, aged 100, still working as a volunteer at the soup kitchen she joined as a 17-year-old, psychiatric nurse writes bestseller and so on
- an anniversary – for example, the world's first test tube baby is 25 today or it's exactly five years since the prime minister came to power
- quiet – there's not much happening, so we'll use that story about the dead donkey.

Sometimes, says Chris Page, there is an almost cyclical element to news:

> There are staple seasonal stories, such as Christmas drink driving, summer holiday safety warnings, school exams and league tables, that come around year in and year out. But we can't keep reproducing the same story and hope that readers won't notice. We need to keep them fresh by introducing new spins, highlighting a new perspective that suggests to readers a new way of seeing an issue or event, rather than relying on tired old formats.

WHO DECIDES?

Who decides what is news? That's easy – the journalist. Most journalists have – or should have – a clear idea of what makes a news story and, therefore, it makes sense that the decision as to whether or not to follow up a news story is left to those who are expert at it – that includes the editor, news editor and reporter. Having said that, it is worth bearing in mind that much depends on the journalist's perception of his or her audience's interests and/or the editor's priorities at any given time.

HOW DOES THE JOURNALIST KNOW?

Some journalists have a 'nose' for news or a 'news sense' and instinctively know what makes a good story. Others have to learn it. As a rule, members of the public do not have this innate sense or feel for news. Nor do they have the benefit of journalism training. A colleague recounts the number of times she has been assailed by members of the public who are determined that what they have to say is 'important news', but it turns out to be something that, although of interest to them personally, will not hold any appeal for a wider audience. It may be that their 'news' has the following flaws:

- It is something that happened a long time ago and so is out of date. News is never about history unless you are putting a 'today' line on a historical event – for instance, 'Papers kept secret for 50 years have been released today and they cast light on ...'
- It is something that occurs regularly and often. The fact that Mrs Helen Smith has risen every weekday morning for the last nine years to take the Number 92 bus to town where she works in a bank is not news. (However, if Mrs Smith was taken hostage, along with all the other passengers on the Number 92 bus, *that* would be news.)
- It is plain boring.

A NOSE FOR NEWS

To reinforce the above point, this same colleague has on several occasions spent time with interviewees who, only as she is about to leave, mention in passing something that has happened or is about to happen to them along the lines of: 'Oh, I don't suppose you'd be interested but ...' When our colleague shows renewed interest, the response is often: 'Oh. I *never* thought you'd want to hear about that ...'

Do not worry if, as a journalism student or trainee journalist, you do not have an instinctive 'nose' for news. Those who do have such instincts are lucky. Those who do not must work at it. One colleague, who teaches part time on a postgraduate journalism diploma course, regularly meets new students who believe that a story is not news if it does not interest them or bores them. She tells them that if it meets the general definition of news, they must develop an interest in it – no matter how briefly. If they cannot become interested in the story they are researching and writing, then their copy will not be interesting to the reader either. In fact, they might not even bother to write a story that, given treatment by another journalist, could make a page lead.

Journalists must learn to recognise the news value of people, events and situations that might otherwise be missed, obscured or simply overlooked by the general public and/or lend interest, meaning and explanation to what can sometimes be dull, tedious and complicated. A nose for news is important, but, having sniffed out a story, a good journalist needs to be able to write it in a way that grabs a reader's attention and, most importantly, holds it.

This is one of the joys of journalism for Adam Wolstenholme:

There is such pleasure to be had in assembling facts and putting them in an attractive, coherent form. I love the whole process of transforming potentially dull material into something highly readable. Glamorous subject matter is no guarantee of a good read. Just look at how boring some profiles of Hollywood stars can be compared to the sort of fascinating stories that can sometimes be drawn from the lives of ordinary folk.

Exercise

Rank the following stories in order of their news value for a large circulation evening newspaper in Yorkshire.

1   A backbench Conservative MP is calling for the resignation of the Labour prime minister.
2   Billions of gallons of water are being lost because of leaking pipes in Sheffield.
3   Sam Bryant, aged 82, was saved by his pet hamster when his Southampton home caught fire two weeks ago.
4   A vote is being taken tonight on plans for a Yorkshire and Humberside Regional Assembly.
5   A former *Big Brother* house mate is opening a supermarket in Leeds tomorrow.
6   A light aircraft has crashed in a field in Kent. The pilot and his passenger escaped uninjured.
7   The Prince of Wales is opening a new art gallery in Newcastle today.
8   Three people have been killed in a street gunfight in Iraq.
9   A form of plastic used to make garden furniture could cause cancer.
10   A Romanian footballer is being signed to play for Leeds United and the club is buying him for a snip.
11   The Secretary of State responsible for housing says more homes are to be built on green belt land in the Yorkshire Dales.
12   The Prime Minister is to unveil a statue in the House of Commons next year.

(Answers are given at the end of the book.)

WRITING NEWS

But Eeyore was saying to himself, 'This writing business. Pencils and what-not. Overrated, if you ask me. Silly stuff. Nothing in it.'

A. A. Milne, *Winnie the Pooh* (2000: 144)

This chapter:

- examines the structure and content of news stories
- explains the important elements of writing news
- discusses the principles of 'KISS and tell', all the 'Ws' and the 'inverted triangle'
- examines what to include in a news story and what to leave out
- explains pegs and angles
- looks at different types of intros
- discusses chronology and when to use it
- looks at quotes and how and when to use them.

To write a news story effectively and well takes skill. There are some journalists who are blessed with an innate sense of how news should be written, but there are many more who struggle at first with the style. Do not worry: news writing is formulaic and, like any formula, can be learned. In fact, learning to write a news story is a bit like learning to cook. The first time a novice chef turns to the pots and pans, he or she opens a cookbook and follows the instructions to the letter. If a recipe calls for two cloves of garlic, two cloves are added. However, experience brings some knowledge of what works and what does not, so, as well as adding the required garlic cloves, the newly competent chef throws in a couple of pinches of mixed herbs, too. News story writing is the same – follow the formula closely until you gain the confidence and experience to know just how much extra spice works for you.

Another way of looking at it is to think of the journalist as an athlete who requires regular practice and coaching to improve. As David Randall (2000: 141), observes: 'Writing is like a muscle, it will be a lot stronger if you exercise it every day.' The more you write, the better you will get.

KISS AND TELL

An important part of the formula is the KISS and tell principle, which has been around for so many years that no one is entirely sure where and how the term was first coined. However, it sums up exactly what a journalist should remember when writing newspaper stories: Keep It Short and Simple – and tell the story. Use short, simple words, phrases and sentences, don't use two or more words when just one will do and avoid long words when a shorter one is available, however authoritative and intellectual the longer one might sound.

> David Todd, assistant editor of the *Sheffield Star*, advises:
>
> Get the facts in the right order and give them to the reader. Don't pepper them with adjectives to try and make things seem more important than they are. Readers buy papers like mine because they want to read about things that are happening in Sheffield. They don't want it presented in a flowery manner. They want the news given to them straight so they can decide what they want to read and what they don't.

ALL THE WS

Another important part of the formula is the list of Ws. Rudyard Kipling wrote the following and it is worth remembering:

> I keep six honest serving-men
> (They taught me all I knew);
> Their names are What and Why and When
> And How and Where and Who. (How is a token W)

A well-written newspaper story will include all the Ws, explaining What has happened to Who, Where and When, How and Why.

INVERTED TRIANGLE

It is a good idea at this point to introduce the inverted triangle or upside-down pyramid – an old-fashioned device the origins of which are unclear, but the rules of which stand the test of time. Think of the widest part of the triangle – the base – at the top and filled with the most important part of the story. The triangle narrows towards the point at the bottom and this is how you must arrange your facts, in descending order of importance. (Every fact should still be accurate, true and interesting.) Imagine a busy sub. He or she has to cut the story. Generally, he or she will start from the bottom up, so it is vital not to bury the crucial part of the story in the final sentence. Using this strategy, a piece will be structured as follows.

The introduction (or intro) at the widest part of the triangle
will contain the Who and the What of the story, plus
perhaps the When?

The next few paragraphs (or pars) will build on the
intro, explaining more of What happened,
How, Where and Why?

Background will be included
to add interest and to put
the story in context.

Finally, loose ends
will be tied up.

WHERE TO START?

At the beginning, of course – except that a news story never starts at the chronological beginning, but, rather, with the ending or the latest, most dramatic or interesting thing to have happened. Journalists, says Lynette Sheridan Burns (2000: 12) 'blurt out something and then explain themselves by attributing each assertion to the evidence of a source with authority to speak on the subject'. Accordingly, while a traditional storyteller would begin: 'Once upon a time, a beautiful girl lived in a big castle with her stepmother and two ugly stepsisters...' and would go on to relate events in strict chronological order, a journalist begins with the information that he or she would blurt out as they rushed through the door of the pub. In this case: 'Prince Charming has announced his engagement to a penniless kitchen maid.'

The idea is that the intro to a story should grab attention and draw readers in so that they read on. For this reason, it is the most important paragraph in the story. It is clear from looking at the inverted triangle on the previous page that getting the intro right is crucial to the structure of a story. The facts and information presented in the intro determine the focus and direction of what comes next. Get the intro right and you will hook your reader; get it wrong and they will look elsewhere. It is worth spending some time, therefore, exploring what makes a good intro.

First, as the inverted triangle demonstrates, an intro must always deal with the outcome of an event – what is the latest, most interesting or most dramatic thing to have happened? However, because news is about people, an intro should also answer the question 'Who?' Who is the story about? You should never write an intro that does not put the focus on people and what has happened to them. The best intros will also answer some of the other Ws, although this is not a priority as the story that follows will expand on the points raised in the intro to include them.

Second, an intro should always be a self-contained summary that, if the rest of the story were to be cut, would be capable of standing alone as a stop press or news in brief (NIB) paragraph.

WRITING INTROS

Sometimes the intro point is obvious. News reports of the death of Diana, Princess of Wales, for instance, almost all began with variations on 'Princess Diana has been killed in a car crash in Paris.' A succinct, direct summary of events that answers both 'Who?' and 'What?'

Most stories, however, are less straightforward. Janice Barker, deputy news editor of the *Oldham Evening Chronicle*, says that if a trainee journalist is struggling, she tells them to think what they would tell their friends about the story if they met in the pub: ' "Well, it's a story about ..." generally leads to a simple summing up just right for an intro.' Often the 'What?' of an intro is obvious but not the 'Who?' In this case, the role of the journalist is to add the human dimension. For instance, a story about a bus crashing into the kitchen wall of a house could start:

> A bus crashed yesterday, demolishing the kitchen wall of a house.

This intro tells you what happened, but not who was affected or involved. A second intro adds a human dimension that helps readers identify with the person involved:

> Part of grandmother Joan Smith's house was demolished after a bus crashed into it.

The third intro, though, goes further:

> Grandmother Joan Smith had planned to spend yesterday baking, but there was little left of her kitchen after a bus crashed into it.

This last intro answers all the questions.

- Who is the story about? Granny Smith.
- What has happened to her? Her kitchen has been demolished.
- Why did this happen? A bus crashed into her house.
- Finally, when did this happen? Yesterday.

More importantly, though, the third example paints a vivid, emotive picture of granny in her pinny, baking buns for the grandchildren – a homely, familiar image with which most readers will empathise.

LAST WEEK, YESTERDAY, WHENEVER, WHEREVER, HOWEVER?

It is not always necessary to include 'When?' in the intro, although it adds to the up-to-the-minute newsworthiness if 'today' can be mentioned.

Working on a regional daily, it is difficult to avoid putting 'yesterday' in an intro as, to a morning newspaper, 'yesterday' or 'last night' is about as up to date as the reporter can be with the news – unless they are writing about something happening 'later today' or 'tomorrow', of course. Likewise, on a weekly newspaper, the news will have been happening 'earlier this week' or 'yesterday' if the events were taking place in the days or day before publication.

Whatever the case, avoid putting 'last week' and certainly, 'a year ago' in your intro as it dates the story, making it *old* rather than *news*. Avoid 'recently', too, as it is too vague.

Tabloids will often ignore both date and place if a story is quirky enough, though, as in this example from the *Daily Mail*:

> Goran Ivanisevic will gladly go where the Williams sisters refused to venture – and spearhead a revolution at the grass roots of British tennis.
> The new Wimbledon champion wants to thank the country for the support he received during 15 days of emotionally draining tennis.

Other newspapers will also disguise the date if the event happened some time ago. In this case, they will update the story in some way to give it a fresh 'today' line. This particularly applies to weekly newspapers covering a significant event that has already been extensively covered in the daily print and broadcast media. So, for instance, early reports in regional evening papers, on the Internet and on the broadcast media about the death of killer Harold Shipman, who, inconveniently for the morning dailies,

was found hanging in his Wakefield prison cell at breakfast time, tended
to be variations on:

> Mass murderer Harold Shipman was found hanging in his cell by prison
> officers this morning.

The *Wakefield Express*, published several days after the event, added fresh
information:

> Britain's biggest serial killer was found by Wakefield prison officers blistered and
> burned when they cut his body down from his home-made noose.

(In case you are wondering, he attached a noose to the bars of his prison
cell and his lifeless body was left dangling against the central heating radi-
ator underneath – hence the burns and blisters.)

Finally, the question of 'How?' rarely needs to be included in the intro
to a first news report of an event. The dailies, of course, unable to tell their
readers about Shipman's suicide until the following day's edition, needed
to be more creative. Thus, *The Guardian*'s report began:

> Just after 6 am yesterday, Harold Shipman, described as a man addicted to
> murder by the judge inquiring into his 23-year killing spree, wound one end of a
> prison sheet round his neck and the other round the bars of his cell and took his
> own life on the eve of his 58th birthday.

A good example of a comprehensive, detailed intro that, most unusually,
answers not only who, what, when and where but also how and, in so
doing, adds a disturbingly pitiful dimension to the death of a man who
might generally be deemed unworthy of sympathy. (The observant among
you will have noticed, too, that, at 53 words, it is also considerably longer
than the recommended 30-word maximum for intros. True, but there is
always an exception that proves the rule. Another exception here will be
found in those tabloid-format regional papers that insist on intros of
between 15 and 25 words maximum.)

MORE ON INTROS
Intros fall into the following broad categories.

Single-sentence intro   This involves some, but not all, of the Ws –
The Guardian's intro quoted above, for instance, is a good, albeit wordy,
example of this type. Generally, a single-sentence intro offers a succinct
way of summing up the whole news story in a sentence. It should contain
the most dominant newsworthy point, as in:

> A boy of 13, accused of murdering his brother by stabbing him with a kitchen knife, today walked free from court.

This intro contains the who, what, how, when and where. It does not offer a why at this stage – that will come later in the story – but it is a potted version of the whole story and arresting enough to make the reader want to read on and find out more.

Two-sentence intro   This is where there are two sentences in a single par. A two-sentence intro is used where the writer has two strong, news-worthy points. So, a report from *The Guardian*'s science editor, Tim Radford, on a new initiative to settle disputes over inherited goods or land begins:

> Economists claim to have found a new way to share the cake fairly. More importantly, everybody will think it fair.

A clothesline intro   This kind of intro is one on which you can hang everything. A clothesline intro contains all the Ws. A much-quoted example is:

> Lady Godiva [who] rode [what] naked on a horse [how] through the streets of Coventry [where] today [when] in a bid to cut taxes [why].

In just 19 words, the writer has given a succinct account that is easily understandable, factual and interesting. Also, there are no complicated words or phrases or unnecessary punctuation to halt the smooth flow of the copy. However, beware. Not all stories lend themselves to a clothesline intro and the danger is that the writer tries to say too much, doesn't say it well and ends up confusing the reader.

Delayed drop intro   This is used to add suspense or surprise. A delayed drop intro involves two sentences in a single or two paragraphs. The first sentence sets the scene, while the second sentence adds a twist. For example:

> The day her daughter was born, Helen Smith was aware of just one person in the packed hospital room.
> It wasn't her husband – but his best friend Tim, the baby's real father.

Another type of delayed drop intro is where the first sentence sets the scene, while the second sentence appears at first to be unconnected. For example:

> Mike Foster will never forget the day he won the Lottery.
> And neither will the local police in the Yorkshire town of Harrogate.

A story with an intro like this will go on to explain what happened to Mike Foster when he won the Lottery – and why the police became involved.

In both these examples, the delayed intro increases the dramatic effect and the reader is sufficiently intrigued to want to know more.

WHO'S SPEAKING, PLEASE?

News stories often hang on the opinion of an important or controversial figure. Nevertheless, it is not modern newspaper style to begin with a direct quote, except on the very rare occasions where the quote might have some special significance. However, the practice of drifting into a quote in the middle of an intro has become distressingly common as in:

> The case of the transplant organs sold over the Internet was described as 'disgusting' by Tony Blair yesterday.

Do not do it. It is a lazy way of writing that frequently produces a weak, wordy intro that holds no real interest for anyone other than the handful of individuals who have a genuine investment in what the Prime Minister may or may not find disgusting.

Instead, summarise the opinions being expressed and use them as indirect speech:

> Furious David Blunkett last night threatened to give police French-style water cannons to blast race rioters off the streets of Britain.

Faced with facts or opinion choose facts first.

Of course, the other point about starting a story with a quote is that the reader will not know who is talking or the context in which the quote is set. The only exceptions might be if the speaker has a distinctive speech pattern, as in this profile of Sir Jimmy Savile in *The Sunday Times Magazine*, which begins:

> 'Now-then-now-then-you-are-asking-me-the-wrong-questions...'

ALSO AVOID ...

... unidentified pronouns in the intro, such as:

> Because he failed his exams ...

as the reader does not know who 'he' is. Also, try not to start an intro with a subsidiary clause, such as:

Delivering oil to Argentina …

as the reader does not know 'who' or 'what' is doing the delivering.

KEEP IT LOCAL

A local or regional journalist must remember that they are writing for a local or regional audience and, therefore, the intro to a news story must carry some local or regional identification. As a result, some newspapers load their news pages with intros that begin: 'A *local* man …', 'A *local* schoolgirl …' or 'A *local* housewife …', which becomes tedious. It is unnecessary, too, as local newspaper reporters would not be writing stories featuring these people if they were not local. Better, instead, to bring in more specific geographical connections, such as 'Residents in a Leeds suburb…', 'A Bristol housewife …' or 'A Manchester businessman…'. Having said that, avoid giving full names and addresses in the intro to a hard news story. Adding a person's name and a street name will only clutter up an intro. Use the name of a person or place the reader does not know or recognise in an intro and there is a strong chance that they will lose interest and fail to read on. As a general rule, leave names until the next par, unless the story is of a lighter nature.

The opposite of this rule applies, however, if the person you are writing about is well known or has celebrity value. For instance, if Prince Charles or David Beckham were visiting your patch, you would use their names in the intro as the names themselves would prove the most interesting draw for your readers.

You can be more specific about the general human interest element of the intro. Rather than say 'A man from Devon…', give more information about the subject – for instance, is he a vicar, judge, businessman or pensioner? Add human interest points like this and a bland, anonymous description becomes more of a picture that the reader can empathise or associate with.

CHECK IT

Having written the intro, check it. Is it concise and simple? Does it read well? Is it accurate? Does it grab the reader's attention? Is it an easily understandable summary of the whole story? Could it stand alone as a single-par NIB? Finally, are there any unanswered questions?

I'VE STARTED, SO I'LL FINISH …

If an intro does its job properly, it will be easier to write the rest of the story using the inverted triangle structure to build on the points made in the intro. The rest of the facts should be presented in descending order of newsworthiness to include an explanation that fills in detail and answers any questions that the reader might have. So, the journalist telling the Cinderella story, having burst through the pub door with the news that Prince Charming is to be married, once he or she had recovered their breath, would expand on the intro:

> A Royal spokesman said they will be married at Leodis Abbey next August. The 28-year-old prince met his future bride, Cinderella Hardup, aged 19, during a winter ball at Leodis Palace.
> The only daughter of the late Baron Hardup, of Hardup Towers, she was disinherited when her father left his fortune to his second wife and her daughters. Since his death four years ago, Cinderella has worked in the kitchens of her former home ...

and so on and so on.

THE WHOLE STORY

A good example of an inverted triangle story is this one taken from the *Nottingham Evening Post*:

> Further talks between Trentbarton bus company managers and its drivers' union have so far failed to resolve a pay dispute.
> Both sides said a meeting at Trentbarton's Heanor HQ yesterday was 'constructive'.
> A further meeting is planned soon in an attempt to reach an agreement and avert further strikes.
> Drivers represented by the Transport and General Workers' Union in the bus company's Trent division staged three Saturday strikes last month.
> Trent drivers want their hourly rate raised from £6.60 an hour to £6.70 or even £7. A pay offer made by the bus company's managers was rejected by the drivers.
> The Barton wing of Trentbarton is not directly affected by the dispute.

The intro answers the questions who and what and could easily stand alone as a self-contained NIB. The second and third pars expand on the points raised in the intro, providing more information about the talks and telling the reader what happens next. The fourth and fifth pars provide background information about what has happened in the past and the final par provides additional information about the scope of the dispute. Finally, because of the way in which the story has been structured, it could easily be cut from the bottom up and the remaining paragraphs would stand up in their own right as a coherent and cohesive report.

Writing a news story is not an exact science. It takes trial and error and a lot of getting things wrong before you get them right. Says Chris Page, editor of the *Selby Times*: 'Getting the facts in the right order is always the hardest part.'

Journalist Holly Smith, of the *Batley News,* agrees:

When I first started, I'd always type up a full transcript of my interview notes. Then I'd go through them, picking out the most interesting bits and I'd scribble a rough draft before I began to key anything in. It was incredibly time-consuming, but I needed to have everything in front of me before I could begin.

In fact, one of the advantages of starting on a weekly is that trainees do have the time to experiment – turnaround times are longer and there is more opportunity to craft a piece rather than simply churn it out. Says David Todd, assistant editor on the *Sheffield Star*:

We've got some very talented young reporters on my paper. They're a lot more confident than people were in my day, which is great, but youngsters who come straight off a course on to an evening paper find that everybody is working at a faster pace. There's less time to offer them help and advice and, because there are more specialists, the opportunities to try different kinds of writing are more limited. On a weekly, trainees will get a much greater variety of work and a much better grounding.

NOT THE INVERTED TRIANGLE

Not all stories lend themselves to the inverted triangle structure. Some are better introduced with background or facts that might not at first seem significant. A good example of this is a report by *The Guardian*'s Luke Harding about an earthquake that devastated the Indian town of Bhachau, which begins:

By 9 am most mornings, the market in the unassuming town of Bhachau is a busy place. Last Friday was no exception. The vegetable seller was putting the finishing touches on his cart, laying out a row of chillies. Mothers were buying shoes for their children. Shopkeepers were chatting and drinking tea. At the primary school, 300 excited small girls were parading to celebrate India's Republic Day. Within minutes, as giant tremors ripped through the lane, almost all of them were dead – drowned under a tidal wave of masonry.

Harding could have begun the story with the information, contained in his second par, that more than 20,000 people died in the earthquake, but his vivid word picture of the town and its people makes the tragic loss of life seem even more acute.

Writing such as this requires skill and practice and, if not done carefully, can become clichéd and trite.

One final point – whichever way a reporter chooses to write the story, it must be readable, fair and accurate.

CHRONOLOGY

Some news stories lend themselves to being told in a chronological way, but not all stories need to be told from A to Z. In fact, it can often help with dramatic effect to move chronological details around.

FACTS, FACTS, FACTS

When writing a news story, stick to the facts and tell each fact one at a time. A helpful rule is to keep to one fact per sentence, rather than layering a story with sentences of multiple and subordinate clauses containing several different facts. Again, the *Nottingham Evening Post* pay dispute report quoted earlier is a good example of this.

A writer should avoid embellishment or the temptation to insert his or her own opinion or comment. If a news story is about the number of deaths caused on the roads by drunken drivers, the reader does not want to read about the writer's personal outrage. They want to hear from official organisations, such as the police, campaigners, victims and perpetrators.

Facts, opinions and comments should all be attributed to a named source.

PEG

A writer needs a peg to hang their story on. This is often connected with a time – for instance, something is happening 'today' – or a location – for instance, something is happening on the newspaper's patch.

ANGLE

The angle is the main slant that the writer is taking with a story – the way he or she is interpreting and approaching the facts contained within it.

CAN I QUOTE YOU ON THAT?

Quotes from a speaker or interviewee bring a news story to life, they add human interest and authenticity. Avoid using quotes simply for the sake of showing that you took a shorthand note. Instead, pick them carefully and they will add weight and colour, offer explanation and help to move the story on.

Quotes are introduced with a colon (:) or a comma (,) and quotation marks – either double (") or single ('), depending on newspaper house style. For style purposes, colons and single quote marks are used in this book.

There are four ways of dealing with a quote:

- as a direct quote
- as an indirect quote
- as a partial quote
- as a statement of fact.

DIRECT QUOTE

A direct quote is one in which you use the speaker's *exact* words, attribute them, introduce them with a colon and place them within quote marks. If you are quoting a speaker for the first time, it is best to introduce them by using their name first. For instance:

Mr Johnson said: 'We heard a loud noise and went to investigate.'

Note that, following the first quotation mark, the first letter is a capital letter (because it represents the start of the quote) and that the full stop is used to end the quote inside the final quotation mark because it is ending the sentence.

Note also that the word 'said' is used here – most newspapers use the past tense although the present tense 'says' can also be found. A reporter needs to check newspaper house style to find out whether past or present tense is used and, whichever it is, use it consistently.

If you have already introduced the speaker, you could write the same direct quote in this way:

'We heard a loud noise and went to investigate,' said Mr Johnson.

Notice that here, a comma ends the quote and then there is a quotation mark followed by 'said Mr Johnson', followed by a full stop which ends the whole sentence.

INDIRECT QUOTE

An indirect quote is where you use the speaker's words and attribute them, but don't put them in quotation marks. Indirect quotes are used to save space and time and summarise what a speaker might have said in a long-winded or complicated way. For instance, if Mr Johnson went all round the houses to tell a reporter about investigating a loud noise, the reporter could summarise it thus: 'Mr Johnson said he had heard a loud noise and went to investigate.'

Note that, although the speaker used the present tense in their actual quote, the past tense must be used in indirect quotes.

PARTIAL QUOTE

Partial quotes are 'snippets' of a longer quote that are used instead of the full quote to save time and space and help summarise. They are attributed and must be accurate and are placed within quotation marks. For example, Mr Johnson said that he heard a 'loud noise and went to investigate'.

Note here that, after the first quotation mark, the first letter is lower case because the word 'loud' is from within the whole sentence, not the beginning of a new sentence in its own right. Note, too, that the full stop comes after the final quotation mark because this is where the sentence the quote is in ends.

In general, try to avoid littering your copy with partial quotes – they are bitty and irritating when overused and the province of journalists with a poor or incomplete shorthand note.

STATEMENT OF FACT

There will be information that a speaker gives you that can be used as fact without reference to the speaker or using quotation marks. For instance, the *Nottingham Evening Post* report quoted earlier includes the statement:

> Trent drivers want their hourly rate raised from £6.60 an hour to £6.70 or even £7.

In this case, it does not matter whether the information came from either drivers or management as both sides agree on the accuracy of the facts.

HE SAID WHAT?

Trainee reporters waste so much time thinking of alternatives for 'said'. They fear that their stories will be littered with 'he said ...', 'she said ...' and so come up with substitutes such as 'commented', 'claimed', 'added', 'went on' and 'remarked'. Think about it though: a short five- or six-par story is not going to carry so many quotes that the word 'said' is going to jar. Also, alternatives such as 'agreed', 'added' and 'claimed' have specific meanings and should only be used to make those meanings clear and in the right context.

Note that 'said' must be used when reporting formal events such as courts, tribunals, public meetings and speeches.

FIGURE THIS ONE OUT

Depending on newspaper house style, numbers one to nine are generally written out in full, while figures are used for 10, 11, 12 and so on.

At the start of a sentence, all numbers should be spelled out – for example:

> Fifteen students left the college early ...

rather than:

> 15 students ...

It is worth checking house style for big numbers. For instance, four million, six hundred thousand and fifteen might look better and be easier to understand in the form 4.6 million.

AGES

Ask someone their age rather than guess or write vaguely that they were 'in their forties'.

Ages are generally presented in stories between commas:

> Tom Johnson, 45, ...

or brackets:

> Tom Johnson (45) ...

but never use both.

Ages at the beginning of a sentence are presented so:

Three-year-old Bethany Johnson ...

note the hyphens and the spelling out of the word three.

CHECK AND DOUBLE-CHECK

It is important to check that all the details of a story are correct, including names, titles and addresses. Never assume that John is spelt with an 'h' – it could be Jon – or that the place name is spelt the way you heard it. You might have heard someone say 'Slowitt', but the name of the northern town they were talking about is spelt Slaithwaite. Check details with your source, in a phone book, on a map or on the Internet.

Always ask interviewees for their full addresses and telephone numbers as you might need to visit or get back to them. Don't, though, print the house name or number (for security purposes) and never give out private telephone numbers unless the interviewee has asked you to and doing so is appropriate for the story – that is, in relation to an appeal of some sort.

Check the rest of your spellings and the grammar.

Check also that you have not libelled anyone in the story or seriously misrepresented them.

Check that the story is balanced. For instance, if you write a story involving person A complaining about the way that they have been treated by person or organisation B, you need to offer a right of reply to B and add B's comments.

The most important point about writing news is to tell the story, says Janice Barker, deputy news editor of the *Oldham Evening Chronicle*:

Confuse the reader or leave him or her to make guesses, bore them because it takes so long to get to the point or not really have a story to tell and you have wasted the reader's time. The story should unfold from an intro which distils the essence of the story without overburdening the readers but encouraging them to read on.

WHAT A NEWS STORY SHOULD CONTAIN

- Angle.
- Peg.
- People.

- Succinct intro.
- Who? What? Where? When? Why? How?
- Short and simple words, phrases and sentences.
- Active voice.
- Quotes.
- Facts.
- Names.
- Ages.
- Addresses.
- Topicality.
- Relevant location.
- Correct spelling and grammar.
- Clear writing.
- Attributable quotes, comments and facts.
- Balance.
- Current, up-to-the-minute and well-sourced information.

WHAT A NEWS STORY SHOULD AVOID

- References to 'me' or 'I'.
- Reporter's personal opinion or comment.
- Passive voice.
- Long words.
- Assumption.
- Speculation.
- Lies.
- Hype.
- Overembellishment.
- Non-attributable quotes, comments or facts.
- Obscurity.

WRITING A NEWS STORY

OK, we have told you *how* to do it, now let's have a go at writing a news in brief, or NIB, news story. The scenario is this: following a bus crash, you have interviewed three people and gathered the information detailed in the panel. Your editor wants an 80–90-word NIB. Where do you begin?

Statement from Chief Inspector George Brown, of Leodis Police

'A man was taken to Leodis General Hospital at approximately 6 am yesterday after the single-decker bus he was driving was in collision with an end terrace property at Balmoral Road, Leodis. Mr Ted Jones, 48, of 72 Windsor Drive, Leodis, sustained minor cuts and bruises but was discharged later the same day. It is understood that he lost control of the bus after encountering a patch of black ice. There were no passengers on board and no charges will be brought against him.

'The householder, Mrs Joan Smith, 67, was upstairs in bed at the time of the collision and did not sustain any injuries, although I understand that she was treated for shock at the scene. Her property sustained substantial internal and external structural damage, but it remains habitable.'

Statement from Mrs Joan Smith, of 21 Balmoral Road, Leodis:

'I'm an early riser and was just about to get up when I heard a loud bang downstairs. I threw on my dressing gown and hurried down to investigate. The kitchen looked as if an earthquake had hit it. There was a hole in one wall and there was dust and plaster and bricks everywhere. It was a terrible shock.

'I don't know how long it will take to sort out all the mess. The wall has been boarded up for now, but the whole kitchen needs rebuilding. The cooker and washing machine were both damaged and I'll need to completely redecorate. I'd set aside the morning to make a cake for my grandson's second birthday party on Saturday, but it could be weeks before I can do any baking in my own kitchen again.'

Statement from Mr Ted Jones, of Windsor Drive, Leodis, a driver for the Leodis Bus Company:

'I left the army a year ago after 15 years as a driver with the mechanical engineering corps. I was unemployed for nearly 11 months before getting this job with the Leodis Bus Company. I've spent about four weeks training and learning the routes and yesterday was the first time I'd taken a bus out on my own. I was on the early morning shift and hadn't even had a single passenger when I accidentally took a wrong turn and ended up in Balmoral Road. It was a cold, icy morning and the bus skidded on a patch of black ice near Mrs Smith's house. I lost control and ended up slamming into her kitchen wall.

'I can't believe that this has happened. I went through the whole of the first Gulf war without getting even a scratch. The first time I take a bus out on my own I demolish a kitchen and end up in hospital.'

WRITING NEWS: THE RECIPE

We said at the beginning of this chapter that learning to write is like learning to cook – except that, instead of a recipe book, we use the inverted triangle or upside-down pyramid structure. Let's recap:

> the intro, at the widest part of the triangle, will contain the who
> and the what of the story, plus, perhaps, the when.

Therefore, keeping the six Ws to the forefront, begin by asking, and answering, the following questions.

- What has happened? A bus has crashed into a house.
- Who has it happened to? Pensioner Joan Smith, whose house has been damaged, and bus driver Ted Jones.
- Why did it happen? The driver lost control of the bus.
- When did it happen? Yesterday.
- How did it happen? The bus hit a patch of black ice.
- Where did it happen? Granny Smith's house in Balmoral Road.

There is no argument about what has happened – there has been a bus crash – but, the fact that there are two possible answers to the question 'Who?' means that the story can focus either on the bus driver or the pensioner. In truth, neither angle is particularly strong. The bus driver story, for instance, boils down to one man being treated for cuts and bruises after a minor collision, while the pensioner story amounts to no more than an old lady's kitchen being damaged. However, a little journalistic spice can turn even the most unpromising material into a good read. So, the intro – a man was treated for cuts and bruises after a bus crash – becomes:

> Gulf war veteran turned bus driver Ted Jones ended up in hospital after taking a wrong turn and crashing into the side of a house.

Alternatively, part of grandmother Joan Smith's house was demolished after a bus crashed into it becomes:

> Grandmother Joan Smith had planned to spend yesterday baking, but there was not much left of her kitchen after a bus crashed into it.

Both now have a sufficiently intriguing human interest angle to persuade readers to ask 'What happened next?' So, tell them. Let's begin with Granny Smith's story.

WHAT COMES NEXT?

As before, use the inverted triangle structure:

> The next few pars will build on the intro,
> explaining more of what happened,
> how, where and why?

What questions, and answers, then, spring from the snippets of information contained in the intro?

- Why was Granny Smith planning to bake? She wanted to make a cake for her grandson's birthday.
- Why did the bus crash into her kitchen? The driver skidded on black ice and lost control of the bus.
- How badly damaged was the kitchen? One wall was partially demolished – fittings and fixtures all damaged.
- Where is her house? 21 Balmoral Road, Leodis.
- When did it happen? At 6 am.
- What did Mrs Smith do? She rushed downstairs.
- What did she see? Her kitchen in ruins.
- Who else was involved? Ted Jones, the bus driver.

Which questions must be answered immediately in order to build on the intro? The accident happened at around 6 am (when) after the driver (who) of the empty bus (what) skidded on black ice (why) and ploughed into her end terrace (where) at Balmoral Road, Leodis.

As a general rule, statements of fact, like those contained in the sentence above, should always be attributed to a named source. However, because there is no disagreement about these details – all three sources provide the same information, albeit in different words – direct attribution becomes unnecessary.

Ideally, too, it would be nice if Mrs Smith's address could be included lower down in the running order as some readers, who either do not know the location of Balmoral Road or who have no interest in what happens in what they consider to be a posh part of town or, perhaps, a particularly seedy area, may be turned off by learning this detail too early. However, because we are writing to a strict word count – 80–90 words – this is the most natural point at which to include this information. It is important, too, to establish that there were no passengers on board – hence, the empty bus, otherwise readers will be curious about not only the fate of the driver, but also that of his passengers.

ADDING BACKGROUND AND DETAIL

We now have the first two paragraphs of a nib that could, if necessary, stand alone. However, we still have a few more words to play with, so let's return to our inverted triangle:

Background will be included
to add interest and put
the story in context.

Back to the six Ws again. What questions, and answers, derive from the additional information we have now provided? In some cases these will be the same questions, and answers, that we considered earlier.

- What did Mrs Smith do? She went to investigate – hurried downstairs.
- What did she find? A hole in the wall and her kitchen covered in dust and plaster.
- What happened to the bus driver? He was taken to hospital suffering from cuts and bruises.
- How did Mrs Smith feel? Shocked.

Put into ordinary language that becomes:

> He escaped with minor injuries, but Mrs Smith's kitchen was in ruins.

Notice that, although it is not necessary to identify the driver (this is Mrs Smith's story, not his), it is essential that we tell readers he was not seriously hurt. Rather than using the formal phrase employed by Chief Inspector Brown, who described him as having 'sustained minor cuts and bruises', it is sufficient to say he escaped serious injury. This is enough information to satisfy the curiosity and natural concern of readers. It is important to reiterate the impact on Mrs Smith's kitchen and, because the word count is tight, we need to summarise the damage rather than go into detail. Describing it as being 'in ruins' provides a mental picture of the impact.

TIE UP THE LOOSE ENDS

This is the next stage of the inverted triangle structure:

> Finally, loose ends
> will be tied up.

Are there any questions arising from the intro or from the supporting paragraphs that haven't yet been answered? Yes, we still haven't dealt with her baking plans. So:

> How do we know that she planned to spend the day baking? Because she told us.

A quote from the main protagonist is often the best way to round off a story and tie up any remaining loose ends. In this case, these are Mrs Smith's wrecked plans to bake a cake for her grandson's birthday. Here we use two short quotes from different parts of her statement to add detail and colour:

'I'd set aside the morning to make a cake for my grandson's birthday,' she said. 'But the kitchen looked as if an earthquake had hit it.'

It is a perfectly acceptable journalistic practice to use quotes in this way, providing, of course, that you do not alter or misinterpret the spirit of what somebody has said. Mentioning her grandson and her plans to make a cake for his birthday add an empathetic human dimension as well as corroborating the intro description of Mrs Smith as a grandmother. Including the line about the earthquake adds colour, emphasising the extent of the damage, and also explains why her little grandson will have to make do with a shop-bought cake.

THE FINAL CUT

We now have a story that reads:

Grandmother Joan Smith had planned to spend yesterday baking, but there was little left of her kitchen after a bus crashed into it.

The accident happened at around 6 am when the driver of the empty bus skidded on black ice and ploughed into her end terrace at Balmoral Road, Leodis.

He escaped with minor injuries but Mrs Smith's kitchen was in ruins.

'I'd set aside the morning to make a cake for my grandson's birthday,' she said. 'But the kitchen looked as if an earthquake had hit it.' (89 words)

It is not, we freely admit, the sort of story that will persuade editors to cry 'Hold the front page!', but it is a tightly written human interest story that should hold the attention of readers from beginning to end. It also comes within the specified word count. A job well done.

Exercise

The news story we have been writing above has two possible angles. It can be told either as Mrs Smith's story, which is the version we've focused on, or as the bus driver's story. Using the alternative intro:

Gulf war veteran turned bus driver Ted Jones ended up in hospital after taking a wrong turn and crashing into the side of a house.

Rewrite the story in no more than 90 words from this second angle using the inverted triangle structure and the six Ws as outlined above.

(Answers are given at the end of the book.)

NEWS LANGUAGE

'I must ask you to not split infinitives,' I said …

'Hear about the bloke who shot the owl?' said Arthur. 'It kept saying to who instead of to whom.'

'Shouldn't it be *Who's Whom* instead of *Who's Who*?' I said …

K. Waterhouse, *Billy Liar* (1978)

This chapter:

- looks at the language of news
- examines how it is written and why it is written in that way
- shows how correct use of language and grammar contributes to understanding and simplicity
- considers colour, house style and headlines
- considers how competition for space, the need for speed and the constraints of newspaper design have affected the language of news
- explores the ways in which news language differs between different print media
- considers how tone and voice affect the choice of language.

Many trainee reporters and journalism students believe that they are going to change the world with their writing style, elegant prose and wide range and understanding of language, but, in the real world of newspapers, there is very little room for the eloquent and elegant form of writing often found in novels. In fact, the celebrated columnist Peregrine Worsthorne (in Glover 2000: 118) makes the rather tongue-in-cheek suggestion that elegance and eloquence are a positive disadvantage. When he started in journalism more than half a century ago, he says, the ability to write was not an important qualification. It was 'even a disadvantage or a liability, since literary facility could so easily tempt a journalist into embroidering the tale which needed, above all else, to be told plainly and unvarnished'.

This is not to say that newspaper writing is somehow a second cousin to the literary variety. Rather, the language of news is a particular discourse with its own vocabulary, style and rhythm that has emerged over time and, while news stories need to be topical, informative, interesting and, sometimes, entertaining, they are generally required to follow a well-defined formula. Good newspaper language is vibrant and explicit, but, most of all, easily understood by the widest possible audience.

STEREOTYPES

Roger Fowler, professor of English and Linguistics at the University of East Anglia, says that newspaper editorials rely on a schema, which he describes as a general term for pieces of tacit knowledge shared by people in a particular community. In other words, he says (Fowler 1991: 4), journalists use stereotypes, clichés and metaphors as a sort of verbal shorthand to add meaning: 'There are always different ways of saying the same thing, and they are not random, accidental alternatives. Differences in expression carry ideological distinctions (and thus differences in representation).' Accordingly, the 'raven-haired teenage temptress' who dates your brother, is not the same person as the 'dark-haired GCSE student' who is carrying his child. The first is a predatory vamp, while the second is the girl next door.

Clearly, every time a journalist chooses one word rather than another, he or she is making decisions about how the facts are presented to the reader and, therefore, how they should be interpreted. Essentially: 'Anything that is said or written about the world is articulated from a particular ideological position: language is not a clear window but a refracting, structuring medium'. (Fowler 1991: 10) Inevitably, however hard a journalist may strive for objectivity, he or she is likely to end up hoist on the petard of value-laden language. In other words, one man's suicide bomber is another man's mass murderer and some poor woman's dead son or daughter.

PLAIN AND SIMPLE

Pragmatically, such subjectivity is unavoidable as journalism cannot succeed in a vacuum: 'Even in what is generally called the "quality" press there is a need to appeal to existing interests and prejudices.' (Cram in Kieran 1998: 163).

Newspapers must pander to the needs and expectations of readers, who, in turn, are loyal to particular newspapers, understand the language and read 'their' newspaper expecting to agree with its comments and opinions. Danuta Reah (1998: 36) suggests that, while there may be no clear profile of a particular newspaper's reader, the papers themselves write as though such a person exists 'and that there is, in fact, a homogeneous group of people with shared beliefs and values whose defining feature is the newspaper that they read'.

Many working journalists would go further, however, and say that a newspaper's readership is not made up of one particular type, but of people from all walks of life and from all forms of educational backgrounds. Furthermore, despite the government's much trumpeted drive to push 50 per cent of the nation's young people into higher education or training, the Plain English Campaign's John Wilde says that the average reading age of the average UK adult is that of a bright nine-year-old. Accordingly, journalists must use language that is common and understandable to all. That language is plain and simple English.

TIED UP IN KNOTS

Unfortunately, too many trainee reporters and journalism students tie themselves in knots with their mission to explain. They overwrite, thus confusing the whole story, which, written simply and succinctly, would convey enough information and meaning for the reader to gain a proper understanding. Take, for example, this intro:

> Leodis' long-term aspirations to provide local teenagers with a venue for socialisation and advice has finally been brought to fruition through the efforts of a dedicated coterie of volunteers who have spent 20 months making over a former town centre laundrette.

It would be much better – because it is tighter and more succinct – written as:

> Volunteers have opened a new advice and social centre for Leodis' teenagers.

You don't need us to point out the obvious differences between these two intros – the first is long-winded, wordy and obtuse, the second plain and direct and, yes, it could have been even plainer and more direct. For instance:

A new teenage advice and social centre has opened in Leodis.

However, we have already explained the need to ensure that every intro answers the question 'Who?' as well as 'What?' More importantly, however, the second example uses the active rather than the passive voice.

LET'S GET ACTIVE

The language of news is busy and active, not lazy and passive. This is one of the most significant differences between the language of news and academic or literary language – and the one that causes most problems for rookie reporters.

A short (simple) grammar lesson becomes necessary here. All sentences require a subject, verb and an object. In simple terms, the subject is the person who does the verb (the doing word) and the object is the person or thing to whom the verb happens. The order in which these three components appear determines whether a sentence is active or passive. So, journalists write:

The man (subject) bit (verb) the dog (object).

This is an active sentence. Academics and literary types, on the other hand, tend to prefer the more passive:

The dog was bitten by the man.

There is a perception – shared, unfortunately, by a regrettable number of students and trainee journalists – that the more wordy a sentence, the more authoritative it must be. This is not the case. Passive sentences are always longer, less direct and harder to understand than active sentences. Newspaper readers do not have lots of time and, if they do not understand something straight away, they will move on to the next story and all your time and effort will have been wasted.

So, never forget: people and organisations do things. Accordingly, start a story, wherever possible, with a noun. For instance:

A Dorset pensioner today hit out at council tax rises …

rather than:

> Council tax rises were today criticised by a Dorset pensioner ...

To take another example:

> The council voted for ...

rather than:

> A vote was taken by the council ...

For most people, it takes time and practice to adopt the active voice as their natural writing voice. Give it time and keep practising.

GO WITH THE FLOW

A well-written news story should read smoothly with easy-to-follow sentences – the reader should not have to keep going back to unpick multiple clauses and work out what is being said.

A well-written story has a rhythm to it that you can hear if you read it out loud. Try it. As you are reading, check for any superfluous words or phrases. Do any of them jar? Are you left in any doubt about what is going on? If so, go back and rewrite the story. If you, the writer, are not clear about any aspect of the story, how can you expect your readers to be?

SHOCK: OVERLY-DRAMATIC ADJECTIVE ALERT HITS SENSATION-STARVED REPORTER IN METAPHOR STORM HYPE HORROR

The shock, horror school of journalism is alive and well and at grave risk of rendering itself meaningless. The overly dramatic use of adjectives, metaphors and hyperbole threaten to devalue news writing. Avoid overstating the case, exaggerating or slipping into a cheap form of tabloidese. For instance, why is it that whenever a sick or injured victim is placed in an ambulance there is a 'mercy dash' to hospital? As Debbie Hall, assistant publications editor for Hull Daily Mail Publications, points out: 'There's no need to overdramatise. If a story isn't dramatic enough in its own right, using flashy words won't make it so. Don't say ambulances rushed to somebody because that's the nature of their job. The news angle would be if they didn't rush.' Also, consider why:

- campaigners 'hit out'
- critics 'slam'
- grannies 'battle'
- police 'probe' or 'crackdown'
- sick babies are 'brave'
- angry people 'fume'
- murders are 'brutal'
- jobs are 'axed'
- salaries are 'slashed'
- pensioners are 'hard hit'
- heavy snow is a 'white hell'
- a heatwave is a 'scorcher'.

It may be that the reporter believes these phrases add urgency and importance to their story, but consider whether or not these are words and phrases in everyday use. For instance, would a 68-year-old pensioner say the following when her pension is accidentally stopped: 'My cash has been axed by those bungling bureaucrats in a tragic funding blunder. I've been hard hit, but I'm brave and battling on in a bid to win a victory over this outrage.' Hardly.

David Todd, assistant editor at the *Sheffield Star*, believes sloppy use of language is a casualty of the cuts in staff that followed the introduction of new technology in the 1980s and 1990s: 'When I trained as a reporter, and later as a sub-editor, there were far more checks in the production cycle before your words appeared in print. If something was below standard or plain wrong, you got it thrown back at you. Now those checks have gone. Newspapers haven't got the people because of the cutbacks.'

Todd has fond memories of one particularly vigilant *Barnsley Chronicle* sports editor called Keith Lodge:

He was one of the first people I worked with and, 20 years on, I still remember the things he taught me. I once did a football report where I used the phrase 'It's been a long week for Barnsley.' He wanted to know what I meant – what was a long week? Was it more than seven days and, if so, how many days was it? Although at the time I thought he was picky, he was right. It *was* a sloppy use of language. A week is a week is a week. He collared me another time when I described the Barnsley squad as being decimated by injuries. It sounded dramatic, but decimated refers to one in ten and that wasn't what I meant at all. Keith taught me a lot about the use of language – most importantly, that if a word doesn't fit, don't use it.

CLICHÉS – THE THIN END OF THE WEDGE

George Orwell (1984: 362) said that clichés were the noises made in the larynx of speakers whose brains were not involved in choosing the words.

Clichés are a particular bête noir of David Todd's: 'They drive me mad. I had a brilliant example the other day where a reporter referred to a university professor as a boffin. What's a boffin, for heaven's sake? It's not a word that people use in everyday language. The guy was trying to make a serious point and describing him as a boffin immediately trivialises it. It's a lazy way of writing.'

Instead, he says, it is the reporter's job to choose words carefully, not fall back on phrases that simply spring to mind:

> Reporters need to police themselves. Clichés are easy to use but, if they are used over and over again, they lose their impact. If you have a column of NIBs that all refer to a car being torched, they lose their impact. People don't use words like that in conversation. I've never heard anybody use the word boffin. If people don't use a word in general language, don't use it.

Furthermore, clichés are hackneyed and trite and a lazy way of writing. Most have lost all expression and meaning. In particular, avoid the following:

- at this moment in time
- to all intents and purposes
- it beggars belief
- the war against inflation
- to be honest with you
- in this day and age
- acid test
- burning issue
- blanket of snow
- it goes without saying
- strike at the heart
- tighten his grip
- few and far between
- even though I say it myself
- pillar (or tower) of strength
- state of the art.

Unfortunately there are many, many more.

METAPHORICALLY SPEAKING

News language teems with metaphors – particularly ones of violence and war, even in peacetime. We commonly read stories where council departments are 'under fire', neighbours are 'fighting bitter battles', jobs are 'axed', grannies are 'battling' and anyone involved in some form of rescue is 'heroic' – come to that, anyone scoring a goal for England, be it football or rugby, is a 'hero'.

Then, in times of war, reporters reload their metaphorical weapons and open fire with a vocabulary that is full of 'Top Gun' bravado. As Britain and its NATO allies readied for the start of attacks on Kosova in 1999, the *Yorkshire Evening Post* presented an extended metaphor in an editorial likening the Kosovo situation, first, to the farming world and then to fireworks. It talked of NATO having 'sown' its 'seeds' (the bombs) with the world now waiting to see what 'harvest' it would bring. However, as soon as the leader writer realised war could hardly be described in terms usually reserved for thanksgiving, he or she left the pastoral for the punchy and moved into descriptions of 'fireworks' in a 'Balkan tinderbox' to describe the light given off by bombs and flares exploding in the night sky.

In fact, metaphors work best when they turn a familiar image on its head. So, for instance, to borrow an example from an unknown Radio 4 interviewee, you might write about someone who has identified a problem but does not have a solution: 'He had the rabbit but didn't have the top hat to go with it.'

The important thing to remember is that, while metaphors can evoke an image that is far more visual than the more factual alternative word or phrase, always use them wisely, carefully and sparingly – with overuse they can turn into clichés (see previous section on this subject).

PUN ME ANOTHER ONE

Be careful with puns. They can work but, unless you are a natural-born comedian, they will not be funny. Also, unless you are a blessed with a vivid imagination, they are unlikely to be original. Particularly tiresome are puns involving:

- cats with nine lives
- boxers/wrestlers up against the ropes
- bankers/Lottery winners coining it in
- tennis players netting cash prizes

- footballers putting the boot in
- singers hitting the right note
- art students having designs on their future
- mountaineers scaling the heights of their ambition
- schools being caned over poor Ofsted results.

SLANG, NEOLOGISMS AND TEEN-SPEAK

Use only when appropriate to the story – and be careful, they can quickly go out of fashion.

EXCLAMATION MARKS OR SCREAMERS!!!

Avoid them in news stories. If one is added to convey meaning, then the story has not been written well enough.

TLAS

Acronyms, or three-letter acronyms (TLAs), should be written out in full the first time they are used in a story with the abbreviation in brackets. Use the abbreviation from then on to save space. Some acronyms are so well known that an explanation is not needed, although an abbreviated form is used in some cases, for instance:

A spokesman for the motoring organisation, the RAC, said …

PARDON MY JARGON

It is very easy to start using someone else's jargon. A reporter, carrying out an interview with, say, military personnel, businesspeople, academics, lawyers or hospital consultants will find that the interviewee uses terms common to their profession. The military man might talk about 'collateral damage', the businessperson about 'thinking outside the box' and the hospital consultant about 'abrasions and contusions'. The reporter must get the interviewee to explain the jargon and then he or she must translate it into everyday language.

When a reporter spends time embedded with the troops on some military exercise or other, it becomes even easier to fall in with the jargon (notice how the term 'embedded' is another piece of jargon that has slipped into common usage). Remember, however, that jargon is often used to make things seem either more or less important than they are (see also the next section on euphemisms). Why else do supermarket shelf stackers describe themselves as 'ambient replenishers' or businesspeople talk about 'downsizing human resources' when what they really mean is sacking people?

It is a skill to resist letting other people's jargon become part of everyday language and use normal parlance to explain what is going on. It is worth remembering that news language is conversational in style and normal conversations carry little in the way of jargon. It is not a sign of a reporter's intelligence to talk loftily about 'dislocated civilian assembly areas', but it is a sign of understanding to talk about refugee camps.

EUPHEMISMS SHOULD PASS GENTLY AWAY ...

... or, rather, die.

Society hides behind euphemisms to make it feel better, soften a blow or avoid confronting reality. Journalists should not. If someone is found guilty of 'terminological inexactitude' or being 'economical with the actuality', they have lied; if they have suffered 'schedule overrun' they are late; if they have been 'restructured', 'rationalised' or 'let go' they have been sacked.

Reporters should say what they mean and that can occasionally involve being blunt. It is not a reporter's job to wrap anything up in cotton wool.

'I'M BEING IRONIC,' HE SAID WRYLY

Newspaper language is not the stuff of Mills & Boon. Interviewees might 'sigh' or 'stifle a sob', but it is not always necessary or appropriate to include this type of linguistic detail.

If a story is written well, the words themselves will deliver emotional impact – it will not be necessary to indicate with the lavish use of adverbs that the person being quoted is being ironic, wry, funny, sad, irritated or angry. Use the favoured way to introduce quotes in news stories, which is: 'He said ...' or 'She said ...'.

WATCH OUT FOR MEANINGLESS MODIFIERS ...

Beware the rather unique situation – if something is unique, it is the only one of its kind so it cannot be 'rather' unique. Keep meaningless modifiers out of copy, along with girls who are nearly pregnant, accidents that are almost fatal and events that are practically impossible. Absolute adjectives are just that.

... AND THOSE THAT DANGLE

Modifiers that are placed in the wrong position in a sentence cause confusion. Avoid them. Here are some examples.

- The protestor was arrested by a policeman wearing nothing but a bath towel.
- The pantomime organisers say children with parents under ten will be admitted free.
- Motorists see plenty of bilingual signposts driving through Wales.

IN SHORT, KEEP IT SIMPLE

Rather than set the pulses racing with an extravagant use of colourful, flowery language, use plain words and phrases. Avoid using two or more words when one will do. Here are some guidelines.

Avoid	Prefer
biggest yet	biggest
meet up with	meet
face up to	face
at this moment in time	now
a large proportion of	much of
draw to the attention of	point out
in view of the fact that	as
made good their escape	escaped
owing to the fact that	because
he was of the opinion that	he thought
with the exception of	except
despite the fact that	although
in the event of	if

Use positive rather than negative words – the glass should be half full rather than half empty – and use concrete, specific words or phrases rather than general or abstract ones. The Edinburgh authorities did not cancel the city's 2003/2004 Hogmanay celebrations because of foul or atrocious weather conditions. Instead, *The Guardian* reports that the cancellation was caused by 'gale force winds' and heavy rain that 'ripped apart tented structures, dislodged masonry and upended ranks of portable toilets'.

Avoid tautology, too. So, aeroplanes do not need to 'circle around' before landing, they simply circle. Similarly, footballers do not 'fall down' when tackled, they fall.

Finally, don't forget [that] the word 'that' can often be omitted from a sentence.

APOSTROPHES

There are plenty of dos and don'ts – and, hopefully, not too many do's and don't's and dos' and do'n't's' – about apostrophes, but it is quite simple. They should be used to:

* mark the possessive – John's coat, the child's bag and the cat's basket
* show that something is missing from a word – it's, don't, can't, won't and haven't.

In general, though, you should never use a short form such as don't or can't in a news story. Always write them out in full – do not, cannot. The only exception is if you are quoting someone directly, as in: 'I can't and won't go there,' said John.

Even so, rookie reporters seem to get terribly confused over the use of your and you're and its and it's. If in doubt, ask yourself, 'Do I mean to write you're going home (as in "you are" going home) or your home (as in belonging to you)?' or 'It's the dog's bone (as in 'it is' the dog's bone) or the dog has its bone (as in the bone belonging to the dog)?' If the grammatically correct version is the longer, more formal 'you are' or 'it is', an apostrophe is required. If you cannot tell the difference between the two, we would strongly urge you to consult *English for Journalists* by Wynford Hicks (1999) and *Eats, Shoots and Leaves* by Lynne Truss (2003) for more on apostrophes and punctuation in general.

ASSISTANT TO THE UNDER-DIRECTOR OF HUMAN COORDINATION (PAPERCLIPS AND STAPLERS DIVISION)

Interviewees, particularly businesspeople, give themselves ridiculously long titles. Avoid being disrespectful to someone's position, but try to shorten long titles if at all possible as they will take up too much space in the story. However, avoid referring to every manager as 'chief', as in 'Health chiefs were meeting today …'.

Also, don't capitalise all job titles. You would not write a Teacher, a Street Cleaner, a Nurse so avoid writing Managing Director with a capital M and D, or Senior Officer with a capital S and O. The exception on some newspapers might include using capital letters for the Prime Minister.

THAT'S ENOUGH OF THAT (ED.)

In-jokes and editorial asides in which the writer makes comments about figures or situations that the reader knows nothing about or addresses the 'dear' reader directly are amateurish and unfunny. They are commonly found in year 10 school newsletters and in-house corporate magazines where inexpert humour, cosiness and the 'good-time-was-had-by-all' style of writing are expected. They do not work in a local or regional newspaper.

COLOUR

When journalists talk about adding colour to a story, they do not mean pictures or purple prose. Colour to writing, like herbs to cooking, should only be added where appropriate and where it is going to add flavour. Reporters generally add colour when they are writing about public events or gatherings, such as at the ornate funeral of a local character or the victory procession through town of the football championship winners. Colour can mean the use of a vivid phrase to paint a picture for the reader, but make it original and avoid going over the top or slipping in too many clichés. For instance, *The Guardian*'s Luke Harding, writing about an earthquake, centred on the Indian town of Bhachau, in which more than 20,000 people died, describes the dead as 'buried under a tidal wave of masonry'. It is an evocative turn of phrase that allows the reader to visualise the powerfully destructive force of the earthquake.

STYLE

While the language of news is instantly recognisable and appears, at first glance, to be common to all newspapers, it is worth noticing differences in style – that is, style as in house style (hyphenation, spelling and other preferences) and manner of writing (how words and phrases are used).

Newspapers differ in the ways that they present quotes, abbreviations, names, ages, titles, capital letters and even swear words. Many newspapers produce their own style books that detail the fundamentals that reporters should stick to, and new reporters and trainees should always ask for a copy.

The style or manner of writing must match the publication and the type of story being written. A reporter should check that the style in which he or she has written a story matches the subject and mood. For instance, a story about a fatal house fire would call for a different style of writing to a feature on ostrich farming; and a court story would have a different style to a golden wedding report.

BE CONSISTENT

The style adopted for a particular news story should be consistent. This advice covers everything from writing in the past or present tense – using 'he says' or 'he said', for instance – how you refer to characters – using just their first name or their full title – or whether the story is being written in a serious or humorous tone.

HEADLINES

Writing headlines is an art form that requires proficiency, confidence and a consummate skill with words. They are written by a sub-editor who will take a reporter's copy and pick out words and phrases that:

- summarise the story – for example: 'City centre sex attack', 'Woman fined for dog mess', 'Yob is banned from city area' (*Nottingham Evening Post* 2004)
- play on words – for example: 'Ramsay cooks up TV show' (*The Mirror* 2004), 'Gene and tonic: science proves that alcoholics can't help it' (*The Express* 2004)
- use a pun – for example: 'Splosh idol' (*The Mirror* 2004).

'Puns are fun,' says Debbie Hall. 'But you've got to be careful that you don't overuse them or be too coarse. One of my favourites was a story about a woman councillor who had a bit of a thing about trying to persuade dog-owners to use pooper scoopers. Of course, the headline to that story just had to be "She scoops to conquer".'

SPACE, SPEED AND DESIGNS ON LANGUAGE

As newspapers have grown in size (consider the number of pull-outs and supplements in the weekend editions alone), the need for more words and pictures has grown. Given the current climate where reporters feel that they must churn out more and more stories, it is worth reflecting on the importance of page design, pictures, illustrations and white space.

A colleague talks about how valuable white space is in a newspaper. What she means is that it can lighten a page and break up columns and columns of black newsprint in just the same way as a clever diagram. This is one of the reasons for newspapers favouring short sentences and paragraphs. They are easy to read and digest and produce the requisite amount of white space. True, it is not the reporter's job to worry about layout, but you will be a better writer if you have an eye for the visual appeal of what you write. For instance, if every paragraph in a story begins with 'a' or 'the', the effect is one of dreary monotony – a message that readers absorb at a very subliminal level. Similarly, if every intro on a page begins with 'A man who ...', 'A woman has ...' or 'The council wants ...' the effect is monotonous.

There is a fine line between creative and imaginative writing that zings with passion and colour and cliché-ridden metaphorical overindulgence – a good reporter strives to walk that line.

Finally, never give in to the temptation to overwrite a story simply to fill a space. If a story is worth just 250 words, write 250 words. Similarly, if your editor or news editor specifies a particular word count for a story, keep to it. If you think it is worth more, discuss it with him or her first. Explain any new facts or angles that have come to light and make your case for giving it more space. Otherwise, it is pointless writing over length copy. Debbie Hall agrees: 'If you're told to do 200 words and then do 300 words, the story will only have to be cut to get it to the right length, which is a waste of your time and the sub's time, too.'

Exercise

Study a local or regional newspaper and count how many clichés, puns and euphemisms you can come up with and then consider alternative words and phrases.

SPECIALIST AREAS - COURT

This country's planted thick with laws from coast to coast – man's laws not God's – and if you cut them down ... d'you really think you could stand upright in the winds that would blow then? ... I'd give the Devil benefit of law, for my own safety's sake.

R. Bolt, *A Man for All Seasons* (2001: 42)

This and the next two chapters look at writing styles and practices within some of the specialist areas of journalism.

- Here, we examine the structure of the English court system and consider some of the skills and specialist legal knowledge needed by a journalist for court reporting.

Many newspapers, especially the larger regional evenings and dailies, have staff whose job it is to cover specialist areas such as court and council reporting. Even so, trainee and junior reporters will find themselves at some time having to do the job. The hope is that the first time you cover a specialist area you will be shadowing a senior reporter who can show you the ropes.

WHY COVER THE COURTS?

The high-minded answer is to echo the sentiments of Sir John Donaldson, later Lord Donaldson, who, giving judgment on the Spycatcher case in the Court of Appeal in 1988, said: '... a free press ... is an essential element in maintaining parliamentary democracy and the British way of life as we know it. But it is important to remember why the press occupies this crucial position. It is not because of any special wisdom, interest or status enjoyed by proprietors, editors or journalists. It is because the media are the eyes and ears of the general public' (Welsh and Greenwood 2002: 1). In short, reporting the courts is one of the bedrocks of our democracy. Essentially, the court reporter is acting as the eyes and ears of the public, ensuring not only that justice is done, but also that it is seen to be done. It is an important function and one that journalists should feel privileged to fulfil. On the other hand, let's be realistic, court reporting remains a staple of newspaper coverage because, as Mark Bradley, editor of the *Wakefield Express* observes, readers lap it up: 'Everybody loves it,' he says.

Bradley's paper reports only the more serious cases in detail, but, like many others, carries a complete list of the names and addresses, together with the charges and penalties imposed by the magistrates, of every defendant who appears before the local bench. It is a hugely popular read. 'For many it's the first page they turn to – people like to look at the list and see their mates, their enemies, their neighbours,' says Bradley.

David Ward, editor of the neighbouring *Pontefract and Castleford Express*, puts it even more succinctly: 'People want to know that Fred down the road has been done for drink driving.'

SEE YOU IN COURT

It can be intimidating to walk through the doors of a court building for the first time – even when you are not the accused – and, indeed, it would be bad practice and irresponsible for a news editor to send a trainee to court for the first time on their own. Typically, you will make your first visit with a more experienced reporter who will explain the geography of the place, outline who the various personalities are and detail the rules – the dos and don'ts.

One colleague remembers how, on her first visit, there was a bewildering number of people moving about the court precincts. The slick-suited man she took to be a solicitor was actually the defendant, the dodgy looking chap in the sheepskin coat was a reporter from another paper and the elderly gent in the flowing black gown, who she took for a QC, was one of the court ushers. As it happens, the latter was the one she befriended and it was he who turned out to be a most useful contact, letting her know in advance of cases coming up and tipping her the wink when a more interesting case was going on in another courtroom.

David Crossland, co-owner of Crabtree's News Agency in Bradford, which specialises in court reporting, remembers his first magistrates' court visit:

> It was a typical local town court with lots of dark oak panelling and a hushed atmosphere. If you have never been in this sort of building before it is awe-inspiring. Nowadays courts go more for light furniture, soft furnishings and subdued lighting. Youth courts, particularly, have been tarted up with low desks and shagpile carpet. I ask, 'When are they going to bring the sweetie jar out so the defendants can help themselves on their way in.'

Another good person to befriend is the court probation officer. They now almost routinely sit in on court hearings in case magistrates request a probation report before determining a sentence. Although many courts make copies of the day's case list, which contains information about defendants' names, ages, addresses and the charges against them, readily available to journalists, they are not obliged to do so. Sometimes, only one copy will be provided, which is fine if you are the only reporter in court, less helpful if the courts are covered by a rival from another newspaper when the rule of first come, first served applies.

Probation officers, however, always have a copy and, in the absence of a media list, friendly ones will often allow reporters to copy down details. They may also have inside information about which cases will go ahead at a particular hearing and which are likely to be postponed. Remember, though, that information on the list should always be checked against anything said in open court. It is not unknown, for instance, for defendants to change addresses between hearings or to have a birthday, making them 25 instead of 24, for example.

Debbie Hall, who covered court for the *Hull Daily Mail* for several years, says that it is a good idea to keep your ears open in the corridors:

> Not because anything untoward is going on, but if, for instance, you hear a bit of hard plea bargaining between two sides, you can get a feel about whether or not a particular case is worth covering and where you will get the best story.

WHAT DO I NEED?

Covering the courts should be treated like any other important reporting job. You should be appropriately dressed and have your notebook, pen (and shorthand) at the ready as tape recorders and cameras are not allowed.

Remember that, even though you are in a courtroom, you are still writing a story. Do not let the legal jargon get in the way of telling the tale. For instance, a court story that begins:

> A woman accused of six charges of possessing ecstasy and amphetamines appeared before Leodis magistrates on Tuesday ...

while technically accurate does not even begin to hint at the human tragedy that turned a single mother into a drug addict facing a possible jail sentence.

Where possible, simplify the jargon. Court references to a road traffic accident or (worse) an RTA may usually safely be shortened to an accident or a crash. Be careful, however, that, in transcribing jargon into everyday language, you do not, for instance, confuse the offence of taking a car without consent (TWOC) with stealing a car – a much more serious offence. Similarly, be clear about the differences between robbery, burglary and theft.

WHAT RIGHTS HAVE I GOT?

Summing up at the end of the Spycatcher case, Lord Donaldson made it clear that the law did not discriminate between journalists and ordinary members of the public. Further, he added: 'Their [the journalist's] right to know and their right to publish is neither more nor less than that of the general public.' (Welsh and Greenwood 2002: 1)

Accordingly, when a journalist reports the work of the courts, he or she has no greater rights or privileges than any other person: '... the journalist, like any other citizen, may legally go anywhere and report anything provided that in so doing he does not transgress the laws of the land, such laws as those concerning theft, trespass, breach of confidence, and defamation' (Welsh and Greenwood 2002: 2). In other words, journalists who break the law will be subject to the same penalties as anyone else. This could have important implications with regard to court reporting as a court report is a news story the whole point of which is to inform readers that somebody has been found guilty of, for instance, shoplifting, and is necessarily defamatory – that is, something that would reduce their standing in the eyes of a right-thinking individual. However, because the law recognises the importance of court reporting in maintaining a healthy and open justice system, court reports, and the journalists writing them, carry an important protection, known as absolute privilege, if what he or she writes is:

- fair – that is, balanced
- accurate and contemporaneous – that is, written for publication in the first issue of the newspaper during or following the court case.

If a story meets those criteria, absolute privilege will protect the reporter from any accusations of defamation.

You must remember, however, that privilege only applies to things that are said during proceedings and not to anything you see or hear, or any interviews you do, outside the court.

REPORTING RESTRICTIONS

A court reporter has to be aware that there are reporting restrictions, some of which are automatic and some discretionary. It is up to you as the reporter to know and understand the law as it pertains to court reporting, so you must be clear about the type of case you are covering and the type of court that it is being heard in. Failure to do so may result in a contempt of court charge – a serious offence carrying substantial financial penalties as well as the possibility of imprisonment.

Remember, ignorance is not a defence. As Dave Crossland says: 'Know your law and be aware – it's not a question of being smart but of self-preservation.'

If in doubt, the best advice we can give is that you refer to the book sometimes called the legal bible for journalists – *McNae's Essential Law for Journalists*. Now edited by Tom Welsh and Walter Greenwood (2003), the book provides a detailed and accessible guide to everything a working journalist needs to know about the law.

CAN I SAY SOMETHING?

As a reporter, you have no rights of address in court, as barristers and solicitors do. However, if the court is considering imposing an order, it will hear representations from the media. If you want to challenge an order, but do not get invited to do so, slip a note to the clerk.

A crown court reporter with the *Newcastle Evening Chronicle* won the right to name a 15-year-old boy who was jailed for life after raping a middle-aged woman. Garry Willey appealed for a Section 39 order not to be imposed at the sentencing of Raymond Stewart at Newcastle Crown Court in June 2003. The order would have effectively banned the identification of the juvenile defendant.

(Continued)

(Continued)

Stewart was just 14 when he broke into the home of a 45-year-old woman and savagely beat her and raped her at knifepoint. Willey says: 'This was a singularly severe case involving an extremely dangerous young man and an offence of such gravity that we felt it was a story we had to cover, and we felt it was in the public interest to name him.'

Willey decided to launch a pre-emptive strike as Stewart's defence team had already told him that they would be applying for the order to be made. Willey wrote to Judge David Hodson prior to sentencing, asking to be allowed to name Stewart: 'It was only a handwritten submission that I passed to the judge via the court clerk, but it set out our reasons and grounds.'

Despite the defence team's objections, the judge agreed not to impose the order. Willey, who has been a crown court reporter for more than a decade, has challenged other orders in the past: 'I find that some barristers and even a few judges are a little hazy on the legislation. They often believe an order is automatic when it is absolutely the opposite. It's amazing the number of times they just assume an order has been made or they forget to apply for one.'

Willey advises reporters not to be scared of challenging orders: 'There is nothing to stop a journalist making a polite and tactful approach to the judge. It's just a question of pointing out what is already in the law books in front of them.'

ORDER, ORDER

There are two (other) important contempt of court orders of which a reporter should be aware:

- Section 4
- Section 11.

Section 4 is a postponing order, where the court can decree that some matters should not be reported for the time being to avoid prejudicing proceedings. For instance, when the judge presiding over the 2003 trial of a businessman, accused of bribing store executives to secure lucrative contracts for his firm, discharged the jury after four days, he issued a Section 4 order to limit reporting of the hearing held in judge's chambers.

Similarly, journalists were prevented from reporting details of a case involving Maxine Carr's mother, Shirley Capp, when she appeared before magistrates accused of intimidating a witness in the Soham murder trial. The order was upheld by Judge John Reddihough at Grimsby Crown Court when Capp, aged 60, appeared before him for a plea and direction hearing in September 2003. However, says Mark Naylor of the *Grimsby*

Telegraph, although journalists were originally banned from publicising the case until after the end of the trials of both mother and daughter, the judge agreed to vary the order in February 2004, following written applications by a number of newspapers and the Press Association. As a result, although the press were still forbidden to mention details of Capp's address or that of the complainant in the case, they were able to report that a committal hearing had taken place.

In this instance, the journalists concerned were in no doubt about the restrictions imposed on them. A word of warning, though, from Adam Wolstenholme of the *Dewsbury Reporter*:

> A recent nasty experience reminded me that you can't rely on court staff to warn you when a reporting restriction is in place. In my first week at my previous paper, they had to stop the press when I discovered at the last minute that there was a Section 4 order on a sex case that I was reporting. There had been no sign up outside court and no mention of this in court by anyone. I only found out about it after pestering the court clerk at the insistence of my news editor. So, my advice to new starters would be: you might not be told about an order. You have to be proactive in seeking them out. In Leeds Crown Court, there is a press room (I now know) that has all the current orders on the wall. Check this and double-check with the clerk. As it happened, the judge had been wrong to make the order anyway as a ban on identifying victims was covered under Sexual Offences legislation, but that wouldn't have saved me.

Section 11 – the other important contempt of court order – is effectively a gagging order that prevents the publication of certain details – the name of a blackmail victim or the address of a vulnerable witness, for instance.

The court should announce if either of these orders is to be imposed, but the onus is on the reporter to find out if they have been. Both orders can be challenged.

MAGISTRATES' COURTS

Most English towns have a magistrates' court, which usually sits every day of the week and deals with mainly minor criminal offences, such as motoring and theft, and some civil matters, such as licensing. More serious criminal cases are referred from the magistrates' court to the crown court. Such referrals are known as committals for trial and, unless reporting restrictions are lifted, a reporter can give only minimum details of such cases, which include the name, age, address and occupation of the accused, the charges against him or her, the names of his or her barrister or solicitor, whether he or she pleaded guilty or not guilty (if a plea is entered), whether he or she was committed in custody or on bail and whether legal aid was granted or not.

KEY FIGURES IN A MAGISTRATES' COURT

The magistrates' court is presided over by justices of the peace, who are unpaid and generally have no legal qualifications, but are advised by a clerk to the justices. Two or three lay justices of the peace sit on what is called the 'bench' in each courtroom. In larger towns, the court may be presided over by a district judge (formerly called a stipendiary magistrate), who is paid and a qualified lawyer and sits on his or her own.

Other key figures in the magistrates' court include the prosecuting solicitor, who gives details of the case compiled from police evidence, and the defence solicitor, representing the accused.

> It is important here to make a clear distinction between solicitors and lawyers or barristers. Solicitors are the people from whom a person accused of a crime will first seek legal advice. They will represent him or her during any appearances at a magistrates' court and, if it becomes necessary, will instruct or brief a barrister to represent the accused at crown court. In fact, their names derive from this practice – a solicitor 'solicits', while a barrister, usually a specialist in a particular branch of the law, practises at the bar, which was originally a partition separating judges from lay people.

FIRST RECOURSE

Magistrates' courts are, in legal terms, courts of 'first recourse'. This means that all defendants, whatever the seriousness of the charges against them, make their first court appearances before lay magistrates. People facing minor or summary offences, such as careless driving, will be tried by the magistrates and, if they are found guilty or plead guilty, will be punished by them.

Other people who have been accused of what are called either-way offences, such as drink driving, may elect to be tried by a jury at crown court or, if they prefer, may elect for summary trial by the magistrates. In most cases, defendants prefer to have their cases heard by magistrates because their sentencing powers, although wide, are not as great as those of a crown court judge. A complete guide to the sentencing powers of magistrates can be found in *McNae* (Welsh and Greenwood 2002: 31–3) but, in broad terms, magistrates may sentence a defendant to no more than six months' imprisonment for a single offence (up to a maximum total of 12 months for more than one offence) or a maximum total fine of £5000. The only exceptions to this rule relate to offences involving customs duty or tax evasion. Crown court judges, on the other hand, may sentence people to much longer prison terms or to much greater fines.

However, magistrates are not obliged to hear cases involving either-way offences. They may decide that the case is too serious – perhaps the defendant was three times over the legal drink driving limit – and instead commit him or her to crown court for trial by jury. Alternatively, having heard all the facts, they may decide that the defendant deserves a greater punishment than they can impose and will commit him or her to crown court for sentencing.

COMMITTAL PROCEEDINGS

The final group of people appearing before the magistrates are those accused of indictable offences. These are the most serious of all – murder, for instance, is an indictable offence – and, in these cases, the magistrates act as what are called 'examining justices'. Their role is to determine whether or not, on the face of it, a case (in legal terms 'a prima facie' case) exists against the accused and, having made a decision, either to commit the defendant to crown court for trial by jury or release the accused and dismiss all charges against him or her.

Usually, both the prosecuting solicitor and the defence solicitor agree on the existence of a prima facie case and the committal proceedings are reasonably straightforward.

Where the prosecution and defence agree on the existence of a prima facie case, the proceedings always follow the same lines. First, the defendant is brought into court and stands before the bench. The magistrates' clerk confirms his or her name, age, address and, sometimes, occupation. The clerk will then put the charge(s) to the defendant and ask whether he or she intends to plead guilty or not guilty. It is rare for a defendant, at this stage, to plead guilty. Usually, they reply 'not guilty' or else the defence solicitor jumps up and informs the court that the defence reserves its plea. Once this happens, either the defence or prosecution will ask for an adjournment to allow time to prepare their case – that is, collect evidence, secure witnesses, complete the paperwork and so on. Such adjournments are usually granted, although the magistrates may quibble a bit if the committal process has been particularly drawn out.

If an adjournment is granted, the chairman or chairwoman of the bench will order the defendant to stand and will tell him or her one of two things:

- that he or she will be remanded on bail until a specified date – this means that the defendant is free to leave the court but will be liable to a substantial financial penalty if they fail to attend their next court hearing

(Continued)

(Continued)

- that he or she will be remanded in custody until a specified date – this means that the defendant is not free to leave the court and will be held in a remand prison until their next court appearance.

If an adjournment is not granted or both prosecution and defence agree that they are ready to proceed, the defendant will be told he or she is being committed for trial to the nearest crown court. Again, he or she will be told whether they are to be remanded on bail or remanded in custody.

Listen out for the words 'remanded on bail' or 'remanded in custody'. Although magistrates sometimes place a defendant on remand for a short period before deciding what sentence to impose, if you hear those particular words, alarm bells should ring – it is possible that you are witnessing committal proceedings and so, beware, reporting restrictions apply.

NO CASE TO ANSWER

Occasionally, the defence solicitor might argue that a prima facie case does not exist and will try to persuade the magistrates to dismiss the charges against his or her client. When this happens, the prosecuting solicitor will outline the case against the defendant and the defence will explain why he or she should not face charges.

This is the point at which committal proceedings become tricky. Although both sides may present their cases in enormous detail, reporting restrictions still apply, except on the very, very rare occasions when one or other solicitor may ask for reporting restrictions to be lifted. In fact, in many years of court reporting, we can recall only one occasion where such an application was made, because the defence hoped publicity would persuade witnesses to come forward to support his client's case.

Unless this happens, do not report anything that you hear in court that relates to what is alleged to have happened. To do so could prejudice a fair trial and then you (and your paper) would be in contempt of court and, possibly, open to libel charges as well.

OTHER REPORTING RESTRICTIONS

There are certain other occasions when reporting restrictions might apply. In a magistrates' court the main restrictions involve sexual offences and young people.

REPORTING RESTRICTIONS FOR SEXUAL OFFENCES

You cannot identify the victim of a sexual offence in his or her lifetime unless the restriction is lifted for some reason by a judge. This means that, unless the judge decrees otherwise, you are barred from giving the victim's name and address, details of their workplace or where they study. Nor can you publish pictures of the victim. You can name the accused, although problems arise where the accused is related to the victim – for instance, in the case of a father raping his daughter.

REPORTING RESTRICTIONS FOR YOUNG PEOPLE

Juveniles aged 17 and under who appear in youth courts as defendants, witnesses or victims cannot be identified. This means that you cannot give their name, address or details of where they go to school. Nor can you publish pictures of them. However, this restriction can be lifted if identifying the accused is in the public interest. For instance, in March 1999 *The Northern Echo* successfully persuaded magistrates in County Durham that they should be allowed to identify the 15-year-old dubbed Boomerang Boy or Homing Pigeon Boy on the grounds that it was in the public interest of the local community to be made aware of the identity of someone who was an habitual offender. Neither they nor other papers, however, were allowed to name the boy's mother or the village where they lived for the sake of his brother and two sisters.

In an adult court, an order has to be made banning the identification of a juvenile, otherwise you can name a young person appearing with an adult.

YOUTH COURTS

Youth courts deal with cases involving young people under the age of 18 and the same reporting restrictions apply as detailed previously regarding the identification and photographing of any young people, whether they are appearing as defendants, witnesses or victims.

CROWN COURTS

Serious criminal cases are referred from a magistrates' court to a crown court, which is presided over by a judge who may be a circuit judge or a recorder.

Crown courts hear cases where the accused faces being sent to prison or where he or she has opted to be tried by a jury.

A crown court jury is made up of 12 members of the public. As a reporter, you are not allowed to report any jury discussion.

If your paper has reported a committal for trial from a magistrates' court, it should also report the crown court trial.

HIGH COURT

Big, interesting and expensive civil cases are heard in the high court, which sits in London and in some larger provincial cities such as Leeds. A high court judge sits on his or her own, although a jury is often called in to decide cases involving libel or slander.

COUNTY COURT

The county court hears less serious civil cases, such as disputes between landlords and tenants, personal injury actions and disputes between neighbours. County courts are presided over by a circuit judge.

If the case is of a minor nature, it could be heard in the county court's small claims court. Decisions here are likely to be taken by a registrar rather than a judge.

CORONER'S COURT

The job of the coroner's court is to hold an inquest to establish how, when, where and why a sudden or suspicious death has occurred.

The coroner is a lawyer or a doctor who sits alone, unless there is serious doubt or the possibility that someone may be criminally responsible for the death, in which case a jury is called in.

A coroner 'records' a verdict; a jury 'returns' a verdict. However, it is not the job of the coroner's court to attribute blame, so there will be no verdicts of 'murder' or 'manslaughter', but instead 'accidental death', 'death by misadventure', 'unlawful killing', 'suicide', 'lack of care' or 'natural causes'. In some cases there will be an open verdict.

Covering a coroner's court requires sensitivity and tact as it is frequently a harrowing experience. However, says David Ward, editor of the *Pontefract and Castleford Express*, it is important not to allow emotions to cloud journalistic judgement:

For you it's a regular experience, but for a witness or family member it can be traumatic. Nevertheless, you've got to maintain a degree of professionalism and switch off and look for the line in the story. No reporter ever forgets their first time in a coroner's court, though. I went on my second day at work with another lad, who was just back from his first NCTJ block release course. We went down to court to cover an inquest into the death of a kid who had been killed in a motorcycle accident. He was only 19. On the way back, the other reporter asked what intro I'd use. I suggested something on the lines of a combination of drink and dangerous road conditions caused the death ... He thought it was a good intro and used it. The accident happened on Scott Hall Road in Leeds and I think about it every time I drive up there.

COVERING THE COURTS

It is important to keep as full and complete a note of the proceedings as possible. Make sure that you correctly record any charges that are put to the defendant(s) and any pleas that are entered. Note the full names of all defendants and witnesses (if any) as well as the names of prosecution and defence solicitors and the bench chairman or chairwoman. Get the age and addresses of defendants (witnesses, too, if appropriate), the decision of the court (whether the defendant was found guilty or not guilty), together with any sentences or fines.

During the hearing, record as many factual details as possible. Listen out for good quotes. A colleague recalls a prosecution solicitor describing the previous record of a defendant as being 'not so much as long as an arm but as long as a leg' – a vivid, graphic description that, please note, was only voiced after the defendant had been found guilty. Neither magistrates nor jurors are made aware of previous convictions until after a decision has been reached.

It can, of course, be difficult to get everything down while proceedings are in progress. Prosecution solicitors, in particular, often speak very quickly and the acoustics of a courtroom, especially older Victorian ones, are not always helpful. Also, the press bench may not always be in the best place to provide reporters with a good vantage point from which to record proceedings.

If you miss anything or are uncertain or unsure about the facts, wait until the court adjourns and ask the prosecution solicitor if you can check details. In our experience, most will be helpful, although some, of course, will not. This is unfortunate, but a good incentive to improve your shorthand.

Defence solicitors are almost universally helpful. From their point of view, having their name and a juicy quote included in a court report is a useful free advertisement. Be sensible, though. Defence solicitors usually leave a courtroom as soon as their client's case has been heard. You can't tap them on the arm in open court and ply them with questions. Instead, follow them discreetly out of court and check any details outside.

Debbie Hall emphasises the importance of making friends of the solicitors and barristers on your patch. The court circuit is a fairly small community in which everyone soon gets to know everyone else:

> You become a familiar face that people get used to seeing around and, if you can build up their confidence and trust and barristers and solicitors know that you will report what they say accurately and spell their names correctly, they'll be happy to give you little snippets and tips. This is especially useful if, like most court reporters, you are trying to cover more than one court at once or if you've got to go out at set times to phone copy through to the office. I've often been told by a barrister to be back in court in ten minutes because something interesting would be coming up. The other benefit of striking up a good relationship is that it also means that you can go to them if you've missed something or if you need to check an important detail. They'll also look after you in other ways, too. I remember in the days before mobile phones that I once had an instance where I had to phone over a story from the court's public call box. The defendant's brother, a great big man with tattoos, very scary, overheard and came over and just cut the line dead. He told me I wasn't going to say anything else about his brother. Fortunately, his brother's barrister came over. He apologised and told him that he couldn't talk to me like that and that I was only doing my job. It was a bit of a wobbly moment though.

WRITING COURT REPORTS

In theory, there should be no difference between writing a court report and writing any other news story as the same basic principles apply. However, in practice, a lot of trainee reporters get very nervous about court reporting. They shouldn't.

The trick is to stick closely to the news writing inverted triangle structure. Start with the most interesting or unusual aspect of the case – often that will be the outcome or the final thing to have happened. In a court story, this is usually based on the fact that person X has been jailed or fined or banned from driving. Accordingly, a typical court intro will be along the lines of:

> Former drug addict Jane Doe escaped jail after magistrates heard how she had turned to drugs to help her cope with a series of personal tragedies.

Note that it is important to establish in the intro that this is a court case, so always include something like 'magistrates were told', 'a court heard', 'at Leodis magistrates' court …' and so on.

The next step is to flesh out the intro just as you would with any other story:

> Twenty-eight-year-old Doe was devastated by the death of her mother after a long illness, closely followed by the break-up of a long-term relationship after she found her partner in bed with another woman.

At this stage the reader should be well and truly hooked and want to read more about a dramatic human interest story. This is the point at which it might be appropriate for you, as the reporter, to establish the exact nature of the charges faced by a defendant and whether or not he or she pleaded guilty or not guilty.

You might, however, want to pile on the drama a bit more:

> She was further rocked by the theft of a diamond ring and other jewellery by the teenage son of a family friend.

At this stage, though, your next paragraph *must* deal with the charges and sentencing. *Never* go beyond the fourth par without making these facts clear:

> Doe, of Leodis Road, Leodis, pleaded guilty at Leodis Magistrates' Court to six charges of possessing ecstasy and amphetamine tablets with a street value of £5500. She was sentenced to 12 months in prison, suspended for two years.

Having established the key facts, you should now attribute them to a named source – initially, the prosecuting solicitor, who outlines the case to the court, followed by the defence solicitor, who presents the defendant's point of view:

> Mr Tom Brown, prosecuting, said the offences were discovered when police, acting on a tip-off, raided Doe's home and found quantities of ecstasy and amphetamines. 'The amphetamines alone, although valued at around £900, were of such a pure quality that they had a street value of £5500,' he said.

Now report the defence case:

> Ms Jane Smith, defending, said Doe was grief-stricken by the death of her mother and the break-up with the father of her three children after she found

him in bed with a woman she had considered a friend. 'The subsequent theft of a ring and other items of jewellery sent her into a downward spiral of chaos that ended with her turning to drugs to help her cope with her multiple problems.'

However, she said that Doe did not deserve to be sent to jail: 'She has overcome her problems and is ready to resume her place as a sensible member of society,' she said.

Finally, end with a quote from the chairman or chairwoman of the magistrates' bench:

Bench chairwoman Mrs Jane Grey said the magistrates accepted that Doe was making a serious attempt to rebuild her life. 'You have had a hard lesson,' she said. 'But we accept that you have no intention of getting involved in drugs again.'

AND FINALLY ...

Debbie Hall advises weaving background information into the fabric of the story. This is especially important with long hearings spread over several days:

You can't assume that readers will have seen the previous day's report and if you tack background information, or a summary of what has gone before, on to the end of a story, there is always the danger that a sub might cut it off by mistake, but if you can weave it into the fabric and keep essential information about the charges fairly high up, there's less danger of that happening.

You've also got to remember to keep the momentum going. Court tends to be dramatic and interesting anyway, but, with an ongoing case, you've got to find a new intro point every day. You can't just regurgitate what has been written before and that can be challenging sometimes if it has been a dull day in court, but I suppose that's part of what makes court reporting enjoyable.

THE SCOTTISH LEGAL SYSTEM

Although the 1707 Act of Union abolished the Scottish parliament – since reinstated by Tony Blair's Labour Government – Scotland has maintained its own distinct legal system, preserving as its principal courts the Court of Session and the High Court of Justiciary. It is a complicated system and we are not qualified to provide a detailed account of its structure or working. Instead, we would recommend to Scottish students and journalists *Scots Law for Journalists* (McKain et al. 2000).

NORTHERN IRELAND'S LEGAL SYSTEM

As with Scottish law, we are not qualified to offer detailed guidance and instruction – we are, after all, journalists and not legal experts. *McNae's Essential Law for Journalists* (Welsh and Greenwood 2002: 435–41), however, includes a chapter on Northern Ireland's legal system that details those areas where administration of the law is markedly different from that on the mainland.

Broadly, the courtroom structure in Northern Ireland is the same as that in England and Wales, with the Lord Chief Justice of Northern Ireland supported by seven high court judges and 15 crown court judges. Unlike England and Wales, however, most cases in magistrates' courts are heard by legally qualified, full-time resident magistrates.

GLOSSARY OF LEGAL TERMS

(adapted from Her Majesty's Court Services website www.hmcourts-service.gov.uk)

Accused	The person charged. The person who has allegedly committed the offence.
Acquittal	Discharge of defendant following verdict or direction of not guilty.
Adjourned generally or sine die	Temporary suspension of the hearing of a case by order of the court. This may be for a short period, such as to the next day, or sine die. Sine die is Latin for 'without a day'. A hearing adjourned sine die stands open indefinitely, without a further hearing having been allocated.
Affirmation	Declaration by a witness who has no religious belief or has religious beliefs that prevent him or her from taking the oath that the evidence he or she is giving is the truth. *See also* Oath.
Appeal	Application to a higher court or authority for review of a decision of a lower court or authority.
Bail	Release of a defendant from custody until his or her next appearance in court, subject sometimes to security being given and/or compliance with certain conditions.
Bar	The collective term for barristers.
Barrister	A member of the bar – the branch of the legal profession that has rights of audience before all courts.

Bench warrant	A warrant issued by the judge for an absent defendant to be arrested and brought before a court.
Bind over for sentence	An order that requires the defendant to return to court on an unspecified date for sentence. Failure to observe this order may result in a forfeit or penalty being enforced.
Chambers	1 Private room or court from which the public are excluded in which a district judge or judge may conduct certain sorts of hearings. 2 Offices used by a barrister.
Circuit judge	A judge who sits in the county court and/or crown court.
Civil	Matters concerning private rights and not offences against the state.
Claim	Proceedings issued in the county or high court. Previously known as an action.
Claimant	The person issuing the claim. Previously known as the plaintiff.
Committal	1 *Committal for trial* Following examination by the magistrates of a case involving an indictable or either-way offence, the procedure of directing the case to the crown court to be dealt with. 2 *Committal for sentence* Where the magistrates consider that the offence justifies a sentence greater than they are empowered to impose, they may commit the defendant to the crown court for sentence to be passed by a judge. 3 *Committal order* An order of the court committing someone to prison. 4 *Committal warrant* Method of enforcing an order of the court, whereby the penalty for failing to comply with its terms is imprisonment. The bailiff is authorised to carry out the arrest and deliver the person to prison or, in some instances, the court.
Common law	The law established, by precedent, from judicial decisions and established within a community.
Compos mentis	Of sound mind – legally fit to conduct/defend proceedings.

Concurrent sentence	A direction by a court that a number of sentences of imprisonment should run at the same time.
Conditional discharge	A discharge of a convicted defendant without sentence on condition that he or she does not reoffend within a specified period of time.
Consecutive sentence	An order for a subsequent sentence of imprisonment to commence as soon as a previous sentence expires. Can apply to more than two sentences.
Contempt of court	Disobedience or wilful disregard of the judicial process.
Counsel	A barrister.
Count	An individual offence set out in an indictment.
Crown court	The crown court deals with all crime committed for trial by magistrates' courts. Cases for trial are heard before a judge and jury. The crown court also acts as an appeal court for cases heard and dealt with by magistrates. The crown court can also deal with some civil and family matters.
Defendant	Person sued or person standing trial or appearing for sentence.
Dock	Enclosure in criminal court for the defendant on trial.
Either-way offence	An offence that the accused may elect be dealt with either summarily by the magistrates or committal to the crown court to be tried by jury. *See also* Indictable offence and Summary offence.
Indictable offence	A criminal offence triable only by the crown court. The different types of offence are classified 1, 2, 3 or 4. Murder is a class 1 offence.
Injunction	An order by a court either restraining a person or people from carrying out a course of action or directing a course of action be complied with. Failure to carry out the terms of the order may be punishable by imprisonment.
Inter alia	Among other things – indicator that the details given are only an extract of the whole.
Judge	An officer appointed to administer the law who also has the authority to hear and try cases in a court of law.

Judgment	Final decision of a court. A monetary judgment requires the payment of a sum of money by one part to another.
Judicial/judiciary	1 Relating to the administration of justice or to the judgment of a court. 2 A judge or other officer empowered to act as a judge.
Jurisdiction	The area and matters over which a court has legal authority.
Juror	A person who has been summoned by a court to be a member of the jury. *See also* Jury.
Jury	Body of jurors sworn to reach a verdict according to the evidence in a court.
Justice of the peace	A lay magistrate – a person appointed to administer judicial business in a magistrates' court. Also sits in the crown court with a judge or recorder to hear appeals and committals for sentence.
Juvenile	Person under 17 years of age.
Law	The system made up of rules established by Acts of Parliament, custom or practice enjoining or prohibiting certain actions. *See also* Common law.
Law Lords	Describes the judges of the House of Lords who are known as the Lords of Appeal in Ordinary.
Legal aid	Facility for the fees and expenses of counsel, solicitors or other legal representatives retained by those of modest means to be paid from a fund administered by the Legal Aid Board.
Libel	A written and published statement or article that infers damaging remarks regarding/affecting a person's reputation.
Lord Chancellor	The cabinet minister who acts as speaker of the House of Lords and oversees the hearings of the Law Lords. Additional responsibilities include supervising the procedures of courts other than magistrates' or coroners' courts and selection of judges, magistrates, Queen's counsel and members of tribunals.
Magistrates' court	A court where criminal proceedings are commenced before justices of the peace who examine the evidence/statements and either deal with the case themselves or commit it to the crown court for trial or sentence. Also has jurisdiction in a range of civil matters. *See also* Stipendiary magistrate.

Mitigation	Reasons submitted on behalf of a guilty party in order to excuse or partly excuse the offence committed in an attempt to minimise the sentence.
Oath	A verbal promise by a person with religious beliefs to tell the truth. *See also* Affirmation.
Plaintiff	*See* Claimant.
Plea	A defendant's reply to a charge put to him or her by a court – that is, guilty or not guilty.
Prosecution	The institution or conduct of criminal proceedings against a person.
Prosecutor	Person who prosecutes.
Queen's counsel	Barristers of at least ten years' standing may apply to become Queen's counsel – QCs. QCs undertake work of an important nature and are referred to as 'silks', which is derived from the court gown that is worn. Will be known as King's counsel if a king assumes the throne.
Recognisance	An undertaking before the court where a person agrees to comply with a certain condition, such as to keep the peace or appear in court. A sum of money is normally pledged to ensure compliance.
Recorder	Also assistant recorder. Members of the legal profession (barristers or solicitors) who are appointed to act in a judicial capacity on a part-time basis. They may progress to become full-time judges.
Remand	To order an accused person to be kept in custody or placed on bail pending a further court appearance.
Silk	Queen's counsel, a senior barrister, sometimes referred to as a leader or leading counsel.
Slander	Spoken words that have a damaging effect on a person's reputation.
Solicitor	Member of the legal profession chiefly concerned with advising clients and preparing their cases and representing them in some courts. May also act as advocates before certain courts or tribunals.
Stipendiary magistrate	A legally qualified and salaried magistrate.
Subpoena	A summons issued to a person directing their attendance in court to give evidence.

Summary offence   A criminal offence that is tryable only by a magistrates' court. *See also* Indictable offence; Either-way offence.

Suspended sentence   A custodial sentence which will not take effect unless there is a subsequent offence within a specified period.

Exercise

Answer the following questions.

1   A justice of the peace is:

   a   a lay magistrate – that is, a person appointed to administer judicial business in a magistrates' court
   b   the person to whom a grant of probate or letters of administration have been issued
   c   a solicitor authorised by the Lord Chancellor to administer oaths and affirmations to a statement of evidence.

2   The term acquittal means:

   a   the temporary suspension of the hearing of a case by order of the court
   b   the release of a defendant from custody until his or her next appearance in court, subject sometimes to security being given and/or compliance with certain conditions
   c   the discharge of a defendant following a verdict or direction of not guilty.

3   The offence of libel concerns:

   a   spoken words that have a damaging effect on a person's reputation
   b   a written and published statement or article that infers damaging remarks regarding/affecting a person's reputation
   c   a written account by a witness of the facts or details of a matter.

4   A bench warrant is:

   a   an order that requires the defendant to return to court on an unspecified date for sentence and failure to observe this order may result in a forfeit or penalty being enforced
   b   a warrant issued by a judge or magistrate for an absent defendant to be arrested and brought before a court
   c   written instructions to counsel to appear at a hearing on behalf of a party prepared by the solicitor and setting out the facts of the case and any case law relied on.

Exercise   (Continued)

5   A barrister is:

   a   a member of the bar, the branch of the legal profession that has rights of audience before all courts

   b   an officer of the county court empowered to serve court documents and execute warrants

   c   someone who is authorised to swear oaths and certify the execution of deeds.

6   A remand order is:

   a   an order attached to some injunctions to allow the police to arrest a person who has broken the terms of the order

   b   a written statement of the charges against a defendant sent for trial to the crown court and signed by an officer of the court

   c   an order that requires an accused person to be kept in custody or placed on bail pending a further court appearance.

7   A subpoena is:

   a   an order following which judgment cannot be enforced without leave of the court

   b   a legally qualified and salaried magistrate

   c   a summons issued to a person directing their attendance in court to give evidence.

8   A suspended sentence is:

   a   a custodial sentence that will not take effect unless there is a subsequent offence within a specified period

   b   the temporary suspension of the hearing of a case by order of the court (maybe for a short period)

   c   the release of a defendant from custody, until his or her next appearance in court, subject sometimes to security being given and/or compliance with certain conditions.

9   A summary offence is:

   a   an offence for which the accused may elect for the case to be dealt with either summarily by the magistrates or by committal to the crown court to be tried by jury

(Continued)

Exercise   (Continued)

    b   a criminal offence triable only by the crown court. The different types of offence are classified 1, 2, 3 or 4, with murder being a class 1 offence

    c   a criminal offence that is triable only by a magistrates' court.

10   A conditional discharge is:

    a   an order for a subsequent sentence of imprisonment to commence as soon as a previous sentence expires that can apply to more than two sentences

    b   a discharge of a convicted defendant without sentence on condition that he or she does not reoffend within a specified period of time

    c   a direction by a court that a number of sentences should run at the same time.

Latin terms are frequently used in court. It is important that you understand what they mean and the contexts in which they are used. Identify the correct meanings of the following terms.

11   Compos mentis:

    a   in good faith – a compos mentis agreement is one entered into genuinely, without attempt to defraud

    b   as a matter of favour – a compos mentis payment would be awarded without the acceptance of any liability or blame

    c   of sound mind – a person who is compos mentis is legally fit to conduct/defend proceedings.

12   Inter alia:

    a   in open court – the hearing of a case before a court sitting in public

    b   among other things – indicates that the details given are only an extract of the whole

    c   ignorance of the law is no excuse – if committing an offence, a guilty party cannot use as a defence the fact that they did so without knowledge that they were breaking the law.

13   Sine die:

    a   without a day – a hearing adjourned sine die stands open indefinitely without a further hearing having been allocated

    b   first sight – sine die evidence would be considered sufficient to prove a case unless disproved and if no sine die evidence can be offered there is no case to answer

    c   in the course of trial – while a court case is under consideration, thus proceedings are sine die and details cannot be disclosed.

(Answers are given at the end of the book.)

SPECIALIST AREAS - COUNCIL

Young Lovell Brown, taking his place for the first time in the Press Gallery of the South Riding County Hall at Flintonbridge ... had come expectant of drama, indignation, combat, amusement, shock. He found boredom and monotony.

W. Holtby, *South Riding* (1981: 21)

This chapter:

- considers some of the issues and problems associated with local government reporting
- looks at the structure of local government
- examines the skills needed by a journalist to cover stories concerning local government.

The local council is an important source of stories for a regional daily, evening or weekly newspaper. Local government decisions affect the lives of your readers and the community in which they live, whether those decisions are about how much council tax is to be levied, where a new school is to be built, if CCTV should be erected on a certain street or where a new bus shelter is to be positioned.

Michael Peel, local government reporter with the *Halifax Evening Courier*, says new and young journalists often dismiss council reporting as boring: 'But it's what you make of it that matters. The difference between council reports and other news stories is the increased challenge to make them interesting, to remove the jargon, ensure political balance and make sure that any opinions expressed are clearly attributed to the relevant politician.'

Peel has been reporting on the affairs of Calderdale Council since it was created in 1973: 'Although the council's powers as a direct provider of services has diminished, its members still have a finger in every pie and their decisions touch every aspect of the daily lives of the people of Calderdale. This leads to a rich source of stories in an area where murders, fatal accidents, house fires and bank robberies are thankfully quite rare.' A cursory glance at some of his stories include such headlines as:

Councillor's threesome
Tory mayor changes sides
Mayor in phone fraud
Tower block demolition
Bridal suite interviews for teachers
Soccer on the rates
Old folks' home closure row.

Boring? Hardly.

WHO SAID WHAT

Nevertheless, local government reporting is not the priority that it was, say, 20 or 30 years ago, when a reporter would be despatched to every minor committee and subcommittee where they would be expected to transcribe detailed accounts of who said what during long-winded debates that amounted to little more than political point scoring.

Today's reports are much more selective, both in terms of content and subject matter. The emphasis is much less on party political issues and much more on how the decisions of council will affect readers. In part, David Todd, assistant editor of the *Sheffield Star*, says that shift reflects different readership priorities – and their palpable lack of interest in town hall politics: 'Look at council voting figures. They're so low now that it is clear readers aren't interested in what happens in the council chamber.'

To some extent, Todd sees this as a matter of some concern: 'It's arguable that we should be making people more aware of what's going on, but it's a chicken and egg situation. We don't cover full council meetings in the same way that we used to do because readers don't want to read about them, but it's hard to know whether or not they might find such stories more interesting if we gave them more space.' On the other hand, he says that papers have to maintain a balance between the sorts of local authority-centred hard news stories that used to predominate and the more human interest, community focused, soft news stories that today's readers prefer: 'Perhaps some of the space that we used to give to council stories has been taken up with what some people might describe as trivia, but we can't have hard news on every page of the paper and you have to remember that the trivial stories are often just as important to readers as a big splash about council tax rates.'

In part, the fact that papers like Todd's no longer prioritise a report of a council meeting above a surprise birthday party for a 100-year-old former farm worker is a reflection of the changing nature of society. On the whole, we are less deferential, less interested in the doings of the great and the good than previous generations. Instead, people are more interested in what is happening on their own doorstep than they are in town hall debates. Not that there are many debates these days. As David Ward, editor of the *Pontefract and Castleford Express*, points out, one of the reasons for his staff rarely covering council meetings is that important decisions are increasingly taken behind the closed doors of party political group meetings rather than in the public forum of the council chamber: 'Plus these days people don't want to know who said what. They want to know what is going on and how much it is going to cost them. They're not interested in reports of bland meetings.'

Jonathan Reed, local government correspondent for the *Nottingham Evening Post*, agrees: 'A lot of the time in the council chamber when councillors get into slanging matches about national issues, you might as well put your notebook away. It's just in-fighting on things that aren't relevant to the local issues that interest readers.'

Some council stories – in particular, those dealing with planning, housing and education issues – can still generate enormous amounts of passion. As Todd says: 'We carry a lot of planning stories, because people get very worked up about them, especially if it is to do with something happening in the city centre. And anything to do with housing is also very important because it affects a lot of people.'

 ## A CYNICAL READERSHIP

To some extent, the lack of interest shown by readers in local government matters is symptomatic of a wider cynicism about politics and politicians. There is a recognition, for instance, that councillors have become adept at manipulating the media to suit their own particular agendas. To some extent this is a problem with any source as all 'cooperate with reporters to the extent that [they] believe they and/or their ideas will gain favourable public access' (McManus in Tumber 1999: 186). Put simply, all sources expect some benefit from cooperating with the press.

Journalists, however, are not stupid and are well aware that politicians have a behind-the-scenes agenda. Indeed: 'It is an iron law of politics that there is always an opposition. Factional tensions and personal hatreds are among the main reasons for significant leaks and any information received should be weighed in that knowledge.' (D'Arcy in de Burgh 2001: 229).

Leaks and tip-offs are the stock in trade of the local government reporter and it is important to be aware of the possible motives of sources and the spin they attach to the information they leak. Says Jonathan Reed: 'Of course, you know that the reason someone is telling you something is because they want to make a political point, but any opposition worth its salt is going to try and highlight the mistakes and incompetence of the ruling party. As a reporter, though, you have to be aware of why people are telling you stuff and take advantage of it – but not to the extent where you are being used.'

In short, you have to keep what Adam Wolstenholme, of the *Dewsbury Reporter*, describes as your news detector in good working order: 'You have to keep a sense of perspective and be prepared to say no.'

However, there is no doubt that sometimes staff shortages and the pressure to generate copy can combine to produce what some describe as a symbiotic relationship between powerful sources of information, such as councillors, and journalists obliged to 'concentrate their resources where significant news often occurs, where important rumours and leaks abound and where regular press conferences are held' (Herman and Chomsky in Tumber 1999: 172–3). Town halls are a quick, easy source of stories and it can be very tempting for lazy reporters to swallow the diet of bland copy being spoon-fed to them.

True, admits Reed:

> If you wanted, you could pick up lots of stories just by going through the agendas and going to the meetings, but it would be deadly dull and you wouldn't be doing the job properly.
>
> Part of the role of a local government reporter is to act as a watchdog and that involves a fair amount of burrowing around and going through figures and accounts and seeing what's worth having a look at. You might have to trawl through quite a lot of very dry stuff, but it's worth it because it is probably one of the most important aspects of the job.

PUBLIC MONITORS

Reed has hit the nail squarely on the head here – and this is reinforced by Mark D'Arcy in Hugo de Burgh's *Investigative Journalism: Context and practice*: 'The local state, in all its manifestations, presents an obvious and legitimate target for scrutiny ... the local media should be ready to pounce on the failure of essential services.' In other words, it is both a duty and a responsibility of a local government reporter to monitor the performance and service delivery of councillors and their paid employees – essentially, to check that council taxpayers are getting value for money.

It is easy enough to do, says Reed: 'A lot of people don't realise that they have a legal right to go through the council's accounts.'

Another useful starting point for an investigative local government correspondent is the Audit Commission's Annual Performance Indicators for local authorities. These 'cover everything from exam results to the efficiency of council tax collection' and 'will give a clear indication when a local authority is falling behind in the standard of service it provides and should prompt local reporters and editors to start asking why?' (D'Arcy in de Burgh 2001: 215). Essentially, the role of an effective local government correspondent is not simply to report what the council does, but investigate what it does not do.

EXPERIENCE MATTERS

Like most specialisms, local government reporting is an area where experience counts. Inevitably, however, while larger daily and evening regional papers can afford to employ experienced, specialist correspondents, regional weeklies may be forced to rely on untrained juniors. This is a problem because all too often they have little idea what is going on or who is speaking (D'Arcy in de Burgh 2001: 215). As a result, they tend to place too great a reliance on council press officers, who, as David Ward observes, are often much older and more experienced, with the result that it is all too easy for them to be fobbed off with anodyne responses. It is the responsibility of editors like him, he says, to not let council staff get away with such fancy footwork and so, although he maintains close personal relationships with both the leader of his local district council and the chief executive. 'I have to make it clear to them that we are not their personal PR service.'

It can be much harder, though, to stop councillors and officials from 'leaning' on younger, less experienced reporters who are much more likely to be a 'prisoner of [their] contacts and become unwilling to antagonise them' (D'Arcy in de Burgh 2001: 229). This is a problem for any journalist, who must always weigh up the short-term gain of a good story now against the loss of future tip-offs. Older hands, such as Michael Peel at the *Halifax Evening Courier* and Jonathan Reed at the *Nottingham Evening Post*, however, experienced in the cyclical nature of journalism, are well aware that yesterday's disaffected source quickly becomes tomorrow's leak, just as soon as they have another hobby horse to ride.

Adam Wolstenholme, of the *Dewsbury Reporter*, advises rookie reporters confronted with a story that is critical of the council – for example, a council house resident whose repeated pleas for help fixing a roof have been ignored – to make sure that they have all the details before approaching the press office: 'They'll fob you off if they can and you can't give them any excuse to claim they are unable to help you.' However, just as councillors are eager to use less experienced journalists to give them good publicity, council tenants are often all too quick to complain to the papers when they have a grievance. As Wolstenholme says:

> Again, you have to be ruthless, otherwise the entire paper would be full of pictures of angry council house residents pointing at leaky roofs or broken toilets.
>
> Incidentally, these stories are one area in which the difference between weekly papers and dailies has been especially marked, for me. I moved from a weekly to a regional evening and my boss at the evening paper was very impatient with stories criticising the council and his advice was to try to get rid of moaning tenants as quickly as possible, unless they had a genuinely newsy story.
>
> Sadly, there's less time to be nice in the more pressured, ruthless atmosphere of the daily paper. At the weekly paper, unless a deadline was looming, I would occasionally let people complain for minutes on end, even after realising that there wasn't a decent story in it, seeing a small part of my job as being that of counsellor for the down-at-heel. No time for that on a busy evening regional.

BOOZE CAMPAIGN

Identifying issues that strike a chord with readers remains the key to successful and effective local government reporting. David Todd, during his tenure as editor of the *Blackpool Gazette*, recognised local unease about boozy holidaymakers drinking in the streets when he launched a campaign to persuade the town's council to introduce a byelaw banning the public consumption of alcohol outdoors. It was a controversial move in a town heavily dependent on tourism: 'I got a lot of stick about it, not least from the people I worked with, but the police were behind it and parts of the council, too.'

Councillors eventually voted in favour of the new byelaw and street boozing is now a thing of the past: 'The campaign succeeded because the majority of our readers were behind it. They were as fed up as I was of seeing the town centre filled with gangs of kids swigging from bottles of beer and lager. The town was much safer for everyone as a result of the new byelaw and, a couple of years later, when there were similar problems in Faliraki, a group of police officers from Blackpool went out to advise them how to deal with it.'

STRUCTURE

The introduction of citizenship classes as part of the Government's reform of the education system should mean that future young journalists have some understanding of how local government operates and how it is structured. However, today's would-be reporters are unlikely to be so enlightened. Most probably cannot even name one of their local ward councillors. (Can you?) Even fewer, we would guess, have a clear idea how local government is structured and who are the key players. So, here follows a brief outline.

Broadly, councils are structured in two ways. In Scotland, Wales and parts of England a single-tier council – unitary, metropolitan or London borough – is responsible for all local authority functions. In the rest of England, there is a two-tier system, in which two separate councils – district and county – divide responsibilities.

In England and Wales, there are 410 local authorities, comprised of:

- 34 county councils
- 36 metropolitan district councils
- 47 English unitary authorities
- 33 London boroughs
- 238 shire district councils
- 22 Welsh unitary authorities.

Metropolitan, English and Welsh unitaries, and London boroughs provide all local authority services to their areas, including social services, education, housing and environmental health.

In areas where the system is split between a county council and a district council, the county provides some services, such as education, social services and trading standards, while the district council carries out others, such as housing and environmental health.

In Scotland, a system of 29 unitary all-purpose authorities is responsible for consumer protection, education, environmental health, fire, housing, leisure, parks and amenities, libraries, planning and building control, police and social services.

DON'T FORGET THE PARISH PUMP

Parish councils should not be forgotten. Too often, there is a tendency to think that parish, town or community councils are so parochial that they do not matter. However, it is the very fact that they are parochial that makes them worth bothering about. Herein lies the stuff of good local news – to say nothing of gossip.

There are about 10,000 parish and town councils in England and community councils in Wales, dealing with matters of local importance, such as lighting, playing fields, public lavatories, seats, shelters and roadside verges.

WHO'S WHO?

To cover the council effectively, as with most of your stories, you need to make good contacts. You will not be expected to know every council member and official personally, but the main players that you need to be aware of are as follows.

- *Councillors*   A local councillor represents a ward – a small area within an authority. There may be more than one councillor per ward. Councillors are not paid, but can claim limited allowances and expenses. Local councillors are a valuable source of stories as they know the area they represent well and are often a first point of contact for members of the public who object to, have problems with or want to raise particular points about local issues, projects and proposals. Michael Peel is on first name terms with all the local councillors in Calderdale, although that doesn't mean he favours one over another:

  > Whenever a politician tries to get his point across, I go to great lengths to get a comment from the opposition. I always try to balance the comments for and against. Fortunately politicians on all sides criticise my reporting at times, which leads me to think that I have the balance about right.

- *Mayor*   Civic mayors, including lord mayors, are councillors who hold what is largely a figurehead position for a year, chairing council meetings and attending civic and community functions. They receive a separate budget for entertainment and running the mayor's office. A handful of local authorities have opted for a directly elected mayor who rules the council like a chief executive.
- *Chief executive*   Chief executives receive a salary, which in itself can provide a topic for stories. For instance, Bradford City Council made headlines in May 2003 when it advertised for a new chief executive with an annual salary of £200,000, which exceeded the £180,000 paid to Kent's chief executive – then the highest paid. By comparison, at the time, the Prime Minister earned £174,414. The chief executive is less concerned with the day-to-day running of the council, concentrating rather on developing policy and systems of management – not unlike the chief executive of a multi-million pound business.

- *Leader* The leader and deputy leader of the council are political appointments based on the number of seats each party holds.
- *Senior officers* Senior officers are professionals, apolitical (as far as the press is concerned) and paid. They include accountants, architects and engineers. Some officers are told not to talk to the press, but those who are allowed to speak can often provide helpful and useful background and facts to a story.
- *PRO* Many councils insist that a journalist goes through the public relations or press office rather than approaching a senior officer direct. PROs should be able to put you in touch with the relevant person, depending on the nature of your enquiry, and they should be able to give you background facts and figures, too. However, experienced journalists, such as Michael Peel, will have built good relationships with their council's chief officers and members with whom they will speak on a regular basis.

JUST A MINUTE

Council meetings are conducted in a formal, businesslike way and items are discussed in a particular order, so you need to learn the structure and process.

Minutes will be sent to your newsroom in advance or will be available on the council website. It is important that these are read carefully as they could provide preliminary stories that might generate local reaction. This gives you another bite of the cherry. A preliminary story might generate letters that will give you a follow-up and it might even persuade members of the public to go to the meeting where the item is being discussed.

THE FULL COUNCIL

A council chamber with a mayor in full regalia and 50 or 60 local politicians seated around the room can be a daunting place for a new reporter, but, in fact, a lot of what happens in a full council meeting is ceremonial, protocol-driven and rubber-stamping. Much of the work has already been carried out at committee stage. However, that does not mean to say that you can take it easy – you need to make sure you know what has been agreed, rejected or referred back to committee and who has said what. Check any decisions or names that you are not sure about with the clerk to the council or a press officer.

A council meeting is chaired by the mayor or a chairperson, who sits near or with the party leaders, their deputies and the chairs of the committee meetings. Members will sit in designated party political blocks.

There will be an agenda and one of the first points on it (after apologies for absence) will be to approve the minutes of the previous council meeting. The meeting will then consider any matters arising before moving on to consider the individually minuted items.

Items on the minutes may be queried with the committee chair and debated. The full council has four courses of action open to it. It can:

- accept resolved items where the committee has been given enough power to make a decision itself
- approve the recommendations made by the committee
- amend a recommendation
- refer the recommendation back for the committee to look at it again.

The press is invited – and, indeed, expected – to attend full council meetings, but the press and public will be asked to leave if anything is to be discussed 'in committee'. This means that the full council itself is going into committee to discuss something of a sensitive, private or personal nature, which it would not be in the public interest to have published.

THE COMMITTEE

Committees and subcommittees consist of small numbers of councillors, usually in proportions relating to the majority and minority parties on the council. However, a committee chairperson is usually elected from the dominant party. All local authorities below county level have committees for highways, housing and leisure services. Some will have ad hoc committees, which are not statutory but reflect the local area – for instance, covering tourism or race relations.

Committee meetings are held in open session and the press is entitled by law to attend them, but reporters might be asked to leave if the members decide to go 'into committee' as with the full council.

Just as the committee is a microcosm of the full council, subcommittees are smaller versions of the committee and discuss specific items in more detail. The press does not have a legal right to attend these meetings.

THE CABINET

Many of the larger authorities now operate a cabinet (or executive) style of local government responsible for most of the day-to-day decisions.

The cabinet (or executive) consists of a leader, who appoints councillors to the cabinet to share leadership of the authority with him or her.

When key decisions are to be discussed or made, these are published in the executive's forward plan. The cabinet (or executive) meets with council officers in open sessions to make decisions, but, where these decisions are outside the budget or policy framework, they must be referred to the council as a whole to decide.

Scrutiny boards support the work of the cabinet (or executive) and the council as a whole and hold public inquiries into matters of local concern – the idea being to allow citizens a greater say.

Scrutiny boards also monitor the decisions of the executive and can 'call in' a decision that has been made by the executive but not yet implemented. This allows them to consider whether or not the decision is appropriate.

AREA COMMITTEES

Some councils have created community involvement teams (CITs), which are area committees responsible for advising the executive and council on matters affecting the CIT's areas. The meetings are held in public.

WRITING COUNCIL STORIES

As with court reporting, always follow the inverted triangle structure. Begin with the most interesting aspect of a story (often the outcome) and lead the reader, step-by-step, through the complexities.

Young or inexperienced reporters often find it hard to settle on an intro. A good tip is to think about how you would explain the story to an elderly relative. How would you summarise the key points in a way that Granny, aged 80, hard of hearing and none too sharp, would find interesting and easily understandable? Thus, an item, drawn from the minutes of the Leodis city centre and south planning subcommittee, features a petition from a bunch of residents opposed to an application to extend a sauna and massage parlour. The petition, which has been signed by 337 people, reads:

> We, the undersigned, object to the establishment of a sex shop at 224/226 Balmoral Road, on the following grounds:
>
> - the use is inappropriate for premises in a local shopping parade area frequented by parents and their families and would amount to a reduction in amenities for residents
> - it will increase traffic and the increase in standing and turning vehicles would be a traffic hazard
> - it will increase crime and fear of crime

- it will harm the status of the residential area
- it will lower the standards of decency
- it will harm community relations
- it will put pressure on other parking areas as visitors will park outside other shops to avoid being seen entering the premises
- premises and staff are likely to be the subject of attacks from the local community
- it will turn the area into a red light district.

REMEMBER GRANNY

There are several interesting issues being raised here – the threat to community relations, the possible threat to property prices inherent in the harm to the area's residential status, the possible threat to life and limb posed by an increase in traffic, the increased risk of crime and, of course, the fear that the neighbourhood could become a red light district.

Clearly, in a typical 300–350-word hard news story it is impossible to deal with all the possible news points. Instead, select those most likely to strike a chord with Granny:

> Worried residents fear they could find themselves living in the middle of a red light district if planners approve a controversial attempt to extend a local sauna and massage parlour.

The intro establishes in a nutshell the who (worried residents) and what (an application to extend a massage parlour), plus why (they don't want to live in a red light district). Strictly speaking, the use of the word 'controversial' is probably a little controversial itself as it constitutes comment – just who has decided the application is controversial? In this case, however, it is pretty clear that this is the opinion of the residents, so it is probably (just) permissible. Note, too, the phrases 'red light district' and 'sauna and massage parlour'. Both have sexual connotations and, we might as well be realistic, sex sells.

BUILD ON THE INTRO

Next, the second, third and fourth pars need to expand and develop the intro, by adding colour and detail:

> And, in a petition to councillors, they warned that local vigilante groups could threaten staff.

> The warning follows an application from the proprietor of The Pampas Rooms in Balmoral Road, Leodis, who wants to expand into adjoining premises.
>
> However, more than 300 people have signed a petition objecting to what they describe as the establishment of a sex shop in a residential area.

The second par establishes that the residents have signed a petition opposing the application and further expands on why they don't think that it is a good idea. Again, note the use of the more informal term 'vigilante groups'. The language of the petition is more formal: 'premises and staff are likely to be the subject of attacks from the local community'. It is, perhaps, a bit emotive to speak of vigilante groups, but, in essence, a community that decides to police its own neighbourhood is taking on the role of a vigilante. In general, there is no problem with colourful language, providing you clarify just exactly what you mean fairly soon afterwards, which we do here.

Remember, too, that news is people, so the focus is on the threat to staff rather than any danger to the premises.

The third par establishes why the residents have been moved to protest – there has been a planning application – and identifies the location of the business at Balmoral Road, Leodis.

The fourth par adds more colour and detail – the number of residents involved in the protests and their fears about the nature of the application and its unsuitability: 'a sex shop in a residential area'. There is an argument for putting the phrase 'sex shop' in quotation marks to make it clear that this is the view of the residents rather than the newspaper. On the other hand, it is clear from the phraseology – 'what they describe as' – whose opinion is being expressed.

PUT THE STORY INTO CONTEXT

Pars five and six go into even more detail about the nature of the protest and specify just exactly what residents have against the proposals and who they hope to influence:

> They hope to persuade members of the Leodis city centre and south planning subcommittee on Monday that a further expansion of the sauna and massage business, in the centre of a parade of shops, is inappropriate in a residential area. They are worried that it will lower standards of decency, potentially turning the neighbourhood into a red light area.
>
> They also fear an increased risk of crime and said that both premises and staff could be the target of attack from disgruntled members of the local community.

It is important that it is clearly established who the residents are petitioning (Leodis city centre and south planning subcommittee) and when (on Monday).

PUT THE OTHER SIDE

So far, we've heard the objections of the residents. The next par begins to present the opposing viewpoint:

> But planning officials, who are advising councillors to approve the extension, have dismissed their concerns as moral scruples. 'A number of objections relate to moral issues. They are not a material planning consideration and therefore should not be given weight in determining this application,' they said in a report to the subcommittee.

Again, we establish whose view is being presented (planning officials), to whom (councillors) and what course of action they propose and why (recommend approval because moral scruples are not a material consideration). Note the mix of indirect and direct quotes – the indirect quote sets the scenario, the direct quote adds weight.

TIE UP LOOSE ENDS

Finally, the last two pars round things off and add a little more detail about why planners feel that they must support the application:

> And, although they conceded that fear of crime could be an important factor, they said protestors had produced no evidence to support their claims. 'Fear of crime is likely to be associated with a number of complex factors, including the physical environment, the lack of activity and surveillance, and it would be difficult to justify a reason for refusal on this basis.
>
> 'In any case, issues associated with any illegal activity taking place on the premises or associated with attacks on people or property are a matter for the police and not the planning authority.'

In an ideal world, the story should also include a direct quote from, for instance, a local community member (perhaps a councillor) or one of the signatories of the petition. In practice, pressure of deadlines might make this difficult. Nevertheless, from a fairly dry and dull planning minute, it is possible to construct a newsworthy and lively story. One that would certainly make Granny sit up and take notice which, and at 327 words, is well within the stipulated word count of 300–350 words.

Exercise

Study the following agenda for the Leodis city centre and south planning subcommittee. Identify which of the agenda items might make a possible news story and what angles you would need to consider.

Agenda

Exclusion of press and public

To identify items where resolutions may be moved to exclude the press and public.

Apologies for absence

Declarations of interest

To receive any declarations of interest.

Minutes of last meeting

Minutes of the meeting held on 4 March 2004.

Leodis Conservation Advisory Group

Minutes of the meetings held on 5 February 2004.

Petitions

- Outstanding petitions list.
  Report of the Head of Development Services.
- Petition requesting road safety measures at Melbourne Road, Leodis.
  Report of the Head of Development Services.

Site visits

- To agree a date for any site visits required in connection with planning applications prior to the next meeting of the Area Board.
- To consider the results of site visits to Leodis Junior Mixed and Infants Primary School, and 21 Wragg View, Leodis.

Proposed closures

- Parts of Albion Road, Leodis.
  Report of the Head of Development Services.
- Part of High Street, Leodis.
  Report of the Head of Development Services.

(Continued)

Exercise   (Continued)

Appeals against refusal of planning permission

- Leodis Dairies: appeal against refusal to extend milk delivery yard at Hensall Road, Leodis, into adjoining green belt land.
- Mr T. Wright: appeal against refusal to allow single-storey extension, plus 24 additional car parking places, at rear of existing supermarket on Woodthorpe Place, Leodis.

(Answers are given at the end of the book.)

MORE SPECIALIST AREAS

The storyteller 'must divine which episodes of (his) history hold promise of fullness and tease from them their hidden meanings, braiding these together as one braids a rope. Teasing and braiding can, like any craft, be learned. But as to determining which episodes hold promise (as oysters hold pearls), it is not without justice that this art is called divining.'

J. M. Coetzee, *Foe* (1986: 88–9)

This chapter:

- considers some more specialist areas, looking particularly at the writing styles and practices of reporters who cover crime, sport, health, business and education.

At some point, most journalists, after a couple of years of general newsroom reporting, gravitate towards one specialism or another. Some, especially those with a leaning towards sport, may have been moving in the direction of a particular specialism from their first day on the job. However, few news editors would encourage a trainee to specialise without first gaining a good general grounding in news journalism because, as Tony Harcup observes in *Journalism: Principles and practice* (2004: 7), 'the fundamentals of journalism must be grasped before more specialised roles can be either accomplished or understood'. In short, although the skills required to be a specialist writer are not particularly different from those of a general news reporter – that is, you need the ability to communicate clearly, write succinctly and with style and to report with tenacity and accuracy – some degree of experience and maturity is also desirable.

CRIME

Crime reporting is exciting and dramatic and about as far removed from covering village fêtes and golden weddings as a reporter can get. The position of crime reporter on a regional evening or daily newspaper is often regarded as one of the most prestigious and exciting specialisms, and the stories that a crime reporter will cover are often the attention grabbers and the front page splashes. However, to a certain extent, the genre is also predictable as there are only a given number of stories that you can expect – although, of course, each one will be different – but the unexpected nature and variety of general reporting is removed.

A crime reporter's main source is the local police force and his or her most important contacts are individual officers willing and able to talk. James Higgins, a crime reporter at the *Blackpool Gazette*, says that a good working relationship is essential: 'Your contacts within the police force are your lifeblood. These relationships are imperative if a newspaper is going to have the exclusives its rivals chase.'

It is of paramount importance, therefore, that the crime reporter is deemed to be trustworthy and reliable. Police contacts will often give you information off the record, but if that off-the-record information is converted into a news story, it is fair to say that the relationship you enjoyed with that officer will be damaged irreparably.

Further, says Higgins:

A crime reporter needs patience in terms of waiting for calls to be returned and, hopefully, contacts will return calls at the first available opportunity, but this will depend on the strength of the relationship you and the officer enjoy.

It's worth remembering that a good working relationship is of mutual benefit. The power of the press is an amazing tool and one that the police will often use to their advantage. Witness appeals through the columns of a newspaper are priceless to officers investigating a given crime and on numerous occasions during my time at the *Gazette* they have proved very fruitful.

Reporters say that they put their own emotions aside when working on a story and this is equally true for a crime reporter, who deals often with emotive issues and has to speak to distraught victims of crime or their families in the most tragic of circumstances. Clouded vision is not an option; the crime reporter must remain focused. This does not mean that you should be unfeeling, but, for the sake of professionalism, your personal thoughts must be set aside.

There are several considerations a crime reporter must take into account when writing – not least the legal aspects of the story. A misjudged article will land not only the reporter in hot water but also, possibly, the editor and the publication, too. James Higgins says that it is also important to remember victims of crime and their families when writing a story: 'In cases involving children or cases where a sex offence has been committed, it is important to ensure anonymity for those involved – another essential aspect of journalism and crime writing in particular.'

It is not a good idea to get too close to your sources. David Randall in *The Universal Journalist* (2000) recounts the tale of a celebrated police reporter with the *Chicago Tribune* in the 1920s whose contacts provided him with a string of well-informed stories about organised crime. He built a legendary reputation with readers and colleagues alike – until he was spectacularly gunned down in 1930 and it subsequently emerged that the reporter, Alfred 'Jake' Lingle, had been systematically exploiting a long-standing friendship with the city's police commissioner to extort money from other policemen wanting transfers and promotions and from politicians, hoodlums and major gangsters, including the notorious Al Capone. It is a story, says Randall, that illustrates the dangers – to both reporter and paper – of a specialist getting too closely involved with sources (Randall 2000: 56–7).

The crime reporter must take into account the fact that he or she will be working on stories involving dangerous and dubious characters. Caution to ensure your own safety is important. Higgins says:

It is often necessary to interview or approach individuals who are less than welcoming and it is a concern, but it is part of my job. With bylines and picture bylines used on a fairly regular basis, journalists are easy to identify. The reality is that, as a local reporter, often living in the community you write about, you are far more accountable to the people who read your product. You tread a fine line every time you write about a person, situation or incident – whether it involves a crime or not – and you must treat every story the same: that is, be meticulously accurate in your approach and execution of the story.

SPORT

A new breed of sports coverage has emerged during the last decade in which the activities of sports people, and their professional and private lives, have moved from the back page to the front of the newspaper. In turn, a new breed of sports reporter has emerged – one who needs a sound knowledge of news and can recognise the difference between stories that focus on, for instance, the financial problems facing a football club, which would go on the front page, and a match report, which would be on the back.

Having said that, knowledge of different sports is essential for a sports writer, although they do not kid themselves that they know everything about all sports. Paul Stimpson, deputy sports editor of the *Cambridge Evening News*, says that what is important when writing about an unfamiliar sport, is to make every effort – via contacts and research – to gain an understanding of that sport so an article can carry the necessary authority: 'Mistakes made through ignorance, or the incorrect use of jargon, will be seen as unforgivable by a contact or knowledgeable reader. In short, you cannot bluff your way through.'

Sports writing is more open to the use of opinion and interpretation than a lot of other genres, says Stimpson:

> Match reports would be bland if they were just a list of facts. As sport is emotional, the writer should be able to convey that emotion and react to it. There is, perhaps, less need to be dispassionate.
>
> Here's a contradiction: the reader knows more about sport than you but the reader knows nothing. That is to say, you may assume a degree of knowledge among readers of the sports pages, but also must be able to write for people who may not have any knowledge of sport. The trick is to get the balance right between not patronising readers and not bamboozling them either.
>
> Also, it is imperative to get the facts right. Readers may disagree with an opinion, but they will respect it, providing the facts behind it are correct. They will, rightly, not tolerate mistakes made through ignorance or sloppiness.

Sports journalism is, perhaps, one of the most significant – and underrated – specialisms in terms of its position within popular culture. Australian communications and media lecturer David Rowe, writing in Dahlgren and Sparks' *Journalism and Popular Culture* (2000 reprinted: 97), describes it as a 'discourse riven with contradiction'. As such, sports writers have to straddle a line between 'the universalism of the Olympian ideal of sport as transcending the routine struggles of everyday life' and the intrinsic competitiveness that asserts 'hierarchical divisions of class, nation, region, race, gender and so on'. On the one hand, sport is a pure celebration of skill and talent; on the other, it is a form of tribal warfare. This contradiction is reflected in the vivid, direct, frequently melodramatic language of sports reporting. Consider, for example, this description by *The Guardian's* Richard Williams (2004) of Pakistan's batsman Inzaman-ul-Haq's valiant stand against the might of India's bowlers:

And when, after an initial flurry of optimism, Pakistan's own innings faltered badly, grandstands that had started the day boiling with exuberant noise gradually fell mute, as if stunned by the 90°F heat. By the time the mighty Inzaman had done his work, however, with a century which deserves to be counted amongst the finest one-day innings of all time, the stadium was once again a cauldron of enthusiasm and the circling predators seemed ready to pick India's bones clean.

To an extent, of course, such language also reflects the stylistic difficulty of reporting week in and week out on what is essentially the same premise: that team A won or lost. As Geoffrey Harris and David Spark point out in *Practical Newspaper Reporting* (1998: 165): 'It is easy enough to report sport adequately; it requires inspiration and great care to report it really well … It needs imagination to grasp the way people feel about their team, the pride they take in a victory.'

The *Cambridge Evening News* devotes an average 46 pages a week to sport, including a 12-page pullout on a Monday. As Stimpson says:

Sport matters to our readers, therefore it matters to us. We concentrate on the local players, from professional level to grass roots, with a healthy helping of national and international sports news thrown in. People want to read about their own exploits and those of their friends, families, colleagues and rivals on, say, the Sunday football scene, about England's top players and every level in between. That is what we aim to give them.

Editor David Ward says his paper, the *Pontefract and Castleford Express*, attracts a lot of readers via the sports pages: 'All the junior sport, since the demise of school sport, is run by local clubs. If we run a report about the under-eights football teams and take pictures of youngsters like little Jimmy scoring a hat trick, parents start buying the paper.'

Paul Stimpson says that he became a sports journalist mostly because he lacked talent for playing sports:

As no England caps or world records are coming my way, watching and reporting other people's exploits is the next best thing. Also, it is a fantastically privileged position to be paid for watching sport. Below top-level sport, giving ordinary people the chance to enjoy a moment in the spotlight by reporting their triumphs and disasters is a good feeling.

BLURRING THE SPORTING BOUNDARIES

When does a sports story move from the back to the front of a newspaper – that is, when does it become a news story? Paul Stimpson says that, broadly speaking, on the pitch is sport, off the pitch is news:

> The latter might include sports players doing other things, supporter misbehaviour, ground development and so on.
>
> Momentous occasions that unite people beyond the local community tend to make front-page news. England's Rugby World Cup win in 2003 is an obvious example, but momentous occasions within the local community similarly go on to the front page – a local professional team winning promotion or a local athlete winning a world title, for example. Even in these cases, the reaction would be on the front, but the action would be on the back pages. There is very little treading on toes between the news and sports departments as long as a little common sense is applied.

HERE'S TO HEALTH

Investigative skills and perseverance are useful tools when dealing with health matters, especially when your sources and contacts are government bodies and NHS management who are suspicious about talking to the media – even when things are going well – and downright obstructive when things are going wrong. A colleague remembers talking to a consultant about the way in which his hospital handled the media during a particular medical crisis: 'We found some reporters skulking in the bushes and managed to fob them off.' Skulking and fobbing is not what dealing with the media should be about at all.

Nor is it about baffling reporters with science. Reporters will find themselves bamboozled by medical jargon. For instance, if a consultant told you that he or she was carrying out a myringotomy, endoscopic nasal polypectomy or fenestration of a cyst, would you have a clue what he or she was talking about? No, of course not, and you are not expected to. Your readers do not know either and, as the reporter, it is your job to explain what these terms mean. This means asking the consultant. Medical people will often object to having such terms simplified as they believe that journalistic simplification is corruption of the information. They also fear being judged by their peers should they appear in the press. It is the job of the reporter to explain that the newspaper is read by a wide audience that includes not just medical experts but lay men and women who have probably never heard some of these terms before.

Persuade the erudite consultant that it is better for him or her to simplify and explain what they mean than for you to have to go somewhere else for elucidation.

The structure of the NHS has changed considerably over the last 30 years and a reporter new to health reporting will need to be sure of the many different parts that go to make up the whole organisation.

ENGLISH HEALTH

The Department of Health has its own press office that reporters can contact, but local journalists will find it more useful to contact the strategic health authority in their region. There are 28 of these around the country, which act as regional headquarters and are responsible for developing plans for improving local health services.

Hospitals are managed by NHS trusts, which are meant to ensure that hospitals provide quality healthcare, and that they spend their money efficiently.

Primary care trusts are local health organisations that manage the services offered by doctors and GPs, dentists, opticians, pharmacists, NHS walk-in centres and the helpline NHS Direct.

There are also care trusts, responsible for health and social care services, mental health trusts, responsible for mental health services, and ambulance trusts, responsible for ambulance services and patient transport.

There are also over 570 regionally based patient and public health forums and their role is to look at health issues locally on behalf of the public.

WELSH HEALTH

The Welsh Assembly Government is responsible for policy direction and allocating funds to the NHS in Wales.

There are 22 local health boards, which assess the health services needed by the population in their area and pay the hospital trusts, family doctors, dentists and so on to provide those services.

There are 14 NHS trusts in Wales, which manage 135 hospitals and include one all-Wales ambulance trust.

There is also a community health council in each of the 22 local government areas in Wales, which take up a wide range of health issues on behalf of the public.

SCOTTISH HEALTH

Scottish health was going through a period of change in 2004. If accepted, proposals in the NHS Reform Bill would see the abolition of the existing Acute and Primary Care NHS Trusts. Trust management was expected to be incorporated into the 15 unified NHS boards throughout Scotland. Each board would have its own press office, which reporters covering Scottish health would be able to contact. The reforms also intended to devolve decision making and resources to frontline staff by establishing community health partnerships.

NORTHERN IRELAND HEALTH

In Northern Ireland, the Department of Health, Social Services and Public Safety provides the umbrella for health services. It includes the fire brigade as well as hospital trusts, community trusts, primary care and ambulance services. There are four health and social services boards for the four regions of Northern Ireland – north, south, east and west – and 19 health and social services trusts, which include acute hospitals, acute hospitals with community services, community services standing alone and the ambulance service.

There are also four health and social services councils – independent watchdog bodies, the role of which is to check that the health service is doing its job. Trusts, boards and councils have regular monthly meetings, which the general public can attend.

HOW HEALTHY IS YOUR KNOWLEDGE?

Madeleine Brindley, health editor at the *Western Mail* in Cardiff, says that to be a health specialist means knowing your subject:

> It's not as though you might be covering a shooting one day and local politics the next. To reporters in the newsroom, you are the expert on health to be called on whenever. You pick up a lot of knowledge about certain medical conditions and illnesses and, saying that, I became a bit of a hypochondriac, worrying about whether I had certain symptoms or would be prone to certain illnesses. It went pretty quickly I'm glad to say.
>
> You also need a strong stomach. I remember one contact – a pioneering key-hole surgeon – who used to show me videos of stomach operations that he had performed. But I have yet to attend an operation.

Brindley's advice to trainee reporters writing on health matters is to remember the reader and check and recheck facts:

When you're writing about waiting lists, new initiatives to boost the number of operations performed, new drugs or whatever, the story must explain how this is going to affect the reader. It's fine writing about the European Working Directive limiting junior doctor hours, or a new consultant contract, but people want to know how that's going to affect them – will it mean hospitals closing, services moving or maybe that they'll have to wait less time to see a consultant?

You also need to be able to cut through all the waffle that the government throws at you – to ignore the fancy dressings and get to the heart of the story. Take waiting lists, for example, in Wales, the Welsh Assembly is very good at pointing out that it has achieved a specific target and ignoring the ever-growing waiting lists elsewhere. It's important to look beyond and find the truth and to be able to ask the awkward questions and, more importantly, get answers.

LET'S GET DOWN TO BUSINESS

A business reporter needs a good head for figures and the ability to understand company accounts because there is often a good story buried within them.

He or she will also need to cut through business jargon – or waffle – to get to the true meaning of what is being said. Joe Watson, business and agriculture editor of Aberdeen's *Press and Journal*, says:

> We may be writing for business, but that doesn't mean we allow the guff of business terminology to appear on our pages. You've also to watch that you're not being used by firms just to give them a free advert. Find out the real truth behind everything you are told, and don't believe a word company PROs tell you.

> Harris and Spark (1998: 146) advise business reporters to insist on being given access to turnover and profit figures as a safeguard against writing a puff piece about a company that subsequently turns out to be struggling: 'Writing about business requires a certain wariness. An apparent success story is not always quite what it might seem. Listen for any snags which, though brushed aside now, could bring damaging publicity later.'

In general, though, there is little difference between writing for the business pages and writing general news. Watson says:

> You are still writing a story that has to be appealing to the reader – and that's the business reader and the general reader. The same premise of who, what, where, why and when is followed, but the best ability a business journalist can have, though, is the one of never giving up and pursuing the truth to the end.

Joe Watson, business and agriculture editor of Aberdeen's *Press and Journal*, was working on a story concerning the collapse of a Morayshire seed potato firm with £10 million debts, which left a small group of dedicated Scottish seed potato growers without any cash for their crops:

> The company managing director left on a holiday to France the day his company went bust and I pursued him to his holiday home in Ceret. He told me how he had lost everything – but not the little white sports car, similar to a Porsche, which was seen at the property. The outcome of the story was that we raised many doubts about his business and he was investigated by the Department of Trade and Industry. That resulted in him being banned as a company director and I won the BT Scottish Business Journalist of the Year award for the stories.

THAT'LL TEACH 'EM

As with any other specialist writer, the education reporter must have the ability to find and recognise a good story, display good fact-gathering and writing skills and produce accurate, balanced copy.

Additionally, as with any other specialism, he or she must know who are the experts and key players, both locally and nationally, and should also have an understanding of the big issues in education. That means knowing the core threads of government and local authority education policy, as well as understanding educational issues specific to their own area and being aware of the concerns of teachers and pupils.

Like many specialists, Anna Davis, education reporter at the *Reading Evening Post*, fell into her current role:

> When I first started at the *Evening Post* I was transport reporter. Then the education reporter left and there was a general shift around of jobs, maybe because certain existing people were getting stale covering the same topic and wanted a change. I think the news editor tried to fit the specialist reporting jobs to people's personalities and specific interests. I don't know how much weight was put on the fact that my partner was just starting a new career as a teacher … but education turned out to be a brilliant subject, which has kept me busy with lots of both off- and on-diary stories.

One of the skills of education reporting is being able to talk to pupils without being patronising. For example, Davis says: 'On results days you have to be down in the schools talking to GCSE and A-level students. You will get better stories if the pupils aren't scared of you and are willing to cry on your shoulder and tell you what they have been through to get their five A grades at A level.'

However, you also need to be able to talk to teachers. Davis adds: 'Sometimes they might treat young reporters in the same way as they treat their own pupils and you will need to be able to stand up to them.'

You also need a thick skin – and, yet, also sensitivity: 'Teachers are extremely protective when talking about their school, especially if you are writing a negative story. You shouldn't be easily fobbed off, but you have to remember that articles in newspapers can have a big impact on a school's reputation and, therefore, on the pupils who go to that school.'

Shahid Naqvi, education correspondent of the *Birmingham Post*, agrees. A story he wrote about a local school bidding for a permanent police office was met with fury. The school claimed that the office was to be sited in an 'education action zone' rather than on the school complex itself, which Naqvi viewed as semantics. Naqvi says: 'They were upset with the negative image that having a police base at the school would send out to the community. Though I stood by my story, their claims that I had done damage to an already deprived and struggling community did hit home and I apologised.'

Naqvi went on to develop a good relationship with the headteacher – he respected the head's passionate protection of his school and pupils. However, the honeymoon period ended when Naqvi covered a serious disturbance at the school. A dispute over a mobile phone led to a group of adults turning up and the situation escalated. 'A number of people – adults and children – were arrested, a 13-year-old boy was hospitalised and four police officers injured,' says Naqvi. 'It was one of those rare things in education reporting – a great live story.' However, when his story appeared, the headteacher complained, objecting to Naqvi's description of the event as a 'riot'. Naqvi says:

Again, I stuck to my story, which, based on the information at the time, I believe was fair, accurate and balanced. The school believed that I had a responsibility to write it in a more positive manner, but, faced with such a dramatic set of events, I believe I would not be doing my job as a reporter if I had played it down. All my gut instincts as a journalist were to tell the drama of the story that had been presented to me – and I would do the same again.

WHERE DO YOU GET STORIES?

Shahid Naqvi has a variety of sources for stories: 'Conferences are good. Education is the kind of area in which there are regular conferences where ideas are expressed and debated. A good story or two is almost guaranteed – and tea and lunch breaks provide a good opportunity to make contacts and even pick up additional stories to follow up.'

As a correspondent, he is bombarded with e-mails and phone calls from people wanting to promote an issue or event:

> Most of these are of minor news value, but, occasionally, there are items that have an angle in them that can be developed into something more interesting.
>
> Council education minutes are worth a look at, too. Unions are a good source of information and, of course, it is vital to have a set of good contacts that you can turn to for advice, quotes and to put a good story your way.

Many of Anna Davis's stories come from parents phoning in and tipping her off – a parent telling her about a teacher whom the parent believes is not acting properly, for instance:

> The best stories are the ones that are interesting to anyone – not just people interested in education. For instance, I have written stories about a school that suffered two arson attacks in two days; pupils who have fought against adversity – like the girl who gave birth to twins just a day after sitting her A levels; and the man who believed his daughter was a genius and wanted the local education authority to pay her fees. I think the best stories are about people – and education is all about people.

Exercise

Take two newspapers – a regional evening and a regional morning. Identify three stories written by three different specialists (you choose which specialities). Now take each of the stories and identify the sources used by the specialist reporter. Consider whether those sources were general contacts, which any reporter might have used, or close contacts of the specialist reporter.

FEATURES

'I don't understand it. What can there be in a simple little story like that to make people praise it so?' she said, quite bewildered. 'There is truth in it Jo, that's the secret; humour and pathos make it alive and you have found your style at last.'

Louisa M. Alcott, *Good Wives* (1983: 246)

This chapter:

- looks at some of the differences between news and features
- examines categories of features and considers the differences between them
- highlights the various styles used in the writing of features.

Many trainee reporters feel that feature writing is not for them. Instead, they prefer the cut and thrust of news.

One colleague, when she was in her 20s and working as a news reporter on a regional daily, viewed the features staff as generally male, older and eccentric. They would place old teapots full of pansies or daffodils on their desks by way of decoration, go out for long lunches where they would amuse each other with their fine phrases and hold literary soirées for a chosen few in their homes – and they all kept cats.

Gradually, however, she realised that there was more to writing features. They gave her the chance to expand on subjects, consider more deeply certain issues and develop her writing style. She now makes a living as a freelance feature writer – and she has never owned a cat in her life.

RULES OF FEATURE WRITING

When it comes to writing features, the same rules apply as for writing news stories. The intro needs to have impact, the feature has to tell an interesting, topical story and it has to have a significant ending.

However, while news tends to be formula-driven, with an inherent speed and urgency to it, features can breathe a little. They are longer – typically between 700 and 1000 words – with a more leisurely pace and structure that allows for more detailed analysis and assessment of people, issues or events than would be appropriate in a news story.

Good feature writers, therefore, require different skills from the news journalist and these are not necessarily ones that come easily to all reporters. Some, for instance, balk at the mere idea of writing hundreds and hundreds of words on a single topic. In a sense, it can be easier for a good reporter to rattle off a 200-word news story about something that is happening right in front of them than produce a 1000-word piece, often based on only one interview.

However, writers find that if the subject of a feature is interesting enough – and they are enjoying writing the piece – the difficulty is keeping within the word limit. Says freelance features writer Carole Richardson: 'That's always my problem and, although it gets easier as you get older and more experienced, I still struggle to keep within a specified word count and get the right level of detail and the necessary twists.'

PEG

As with news stories, a feature must have a reason for being printed and this is the peg that it hangs on. The peg is commonly connected with time and can often be something as simple as the fact that something is happening or has happened or will happen 'this week' or 'this month'.

However, while the peg for a news story will usually be contained in the intro, a feature peg may not become apparent until the second, third or even the fourth or fifth par. At other times, the peg might not have anything approaching a news angle. Instead, the peg might be tied to something quirky or unusual about the individuals being featured.

INTEREST, FOCUS AND PURPOSE

Regardless of the peg, a journalist must ask him- or herself if there is enough mileage in the subject to make it interesting enough to sustain the extra word length of a feature. Answering that question, though, requires that you know the answers to two further questions: who are my readers and why am I writing about this subject? Both are crucial to effective feature writing, says Carole Richardson. Most publications have a detailed readership profile (they use them to sell advertising) and, as a freelance, she familiarises herself with them to help build up a picture of a typical reader: 'It helps me find something that readers can identify with.'

You also need to be clear about the purpose of a feature – whether it is entertainment, information or education. Often it might be a mix of all three, but you need to know before you start writing what you want your readers to take away from the piece.

ANGLE

As we said in Chapter 3, Writing News, the angle is the main slant that the writer is taking or the theme that he or she is following – in short, the way he or she is interpreting and approaching the facts. Is it appropriate for the subject matter? Is it one that the reader will find interesting? In most cases, such decisions will not be down to you as a writer. Instead, your editor or news editor will have determined the angle beforehand. Says Richardson: 'A lot of the time I get told that one sort of theme or another is needed. It helps me frame my questions to tease out the information I need to write the piece that the news editor wants.'

Sometimes, of course, an interview does not follow the expected path – quite simply, the facts you elicit do not support the theme or angle pre-ordained by an editor or news editor. It is not a good idea to try and make the facts fit – simply get as much information as you can and, back at the newsroom, explain why the feature does not stand up and suggest alternative angles or scenarios.

TONE

The tone or voice of a feature must reflect its subject. For instance, is it going to be serious, table-thumping, entertaining or humorous? Most reporters, as they become more experienced at writing features, often develop a flair for writing in a particular voice. Some are better at the table-thumping stuff, while others have a naturally light touch. To some extent, the voice in which you write is likely to reflect your individual personality – somebody who is naturally serious-minded and thoughtful will find it harder to write an amusing, light-hearted piece than someone with a more effervescent personality. This is not a problem as every writer should play to their strengths and, although your editor or news editor will indicate what tone they expect a feature to take, they will have considered your writing style when they commissioned you or selected you for an assignment.

THE INTRO

As with a news story, the intro is the most important part of the feature and should be interesting and arresting enough to make the reader want to read on. In a news story, it is important to get to the point quickly, but, says Debbie Hall – who is responsible for producing specialist feature supplements for Hull Daily Mail Publications – features allow writers more opportunity to be creative:

> In a feature you can sometimes get away with teasing people a bit because you know that you've got more space and it won't be cut, so, sometimes, a delayed intro works well. One of my favourites was a story I did about a couple of cheesemakers who made goats' cheese. One of the interesting things I found out was the fact that they used towelling nappies to drain their cheese because it was the most absorbent material. So my intro was all about their sleepless nights and nappy changing. I didn't get to the real point until some way down.

Feature writers are told to avoid starting a feature with a quote. The reader does not know who is speaking and, unless the words are familiar – for instance, from a well-known speech by a well-known personality or character, such as a politician – they will not know what the subject is about either. However, the technique can work, as this example from the *Eastern Daily Press* shows:

> 'Don't treat me like an idiot,' the Princess told Camilla Parker Bowles. 'I know what is going on between you and Charles and I just want you to know that.'

The quote is totally appropriate, given that the feature was written in response to the broadcasting in the United States of secretly recorded tapes made by Princess Diana during the break-up of her marriage. The opening quote is lifted from the tapes and the speaker and the person to whom she is speaking are instantly recognisable.

Reporters are told to avoid starting a news story with an unidentified pronoun – for much the same reason that they are advised to avoid starting a news story with a quote. However, some feature writers are able to add intrigue by doing exactly that – as the following example from the

Yorkshire Evening Post shows in a profile feature about the leader of an orchestra:

> As he takes his seat in the darkened orchestra pit his mind is focused on the evening's performance. It could be one of six operas in the current season's repertoire at any one of half a dozen theatres.

The style of writing, in setting the scene and posing the question as to where this is happening, intrigues the reader and makes him or her want to read on to find out who 'he' is.

Some intros are written with such imaginative enthusiasm that they have the effect of pulling the reader right into the action – as in this example from the *Lancashire Evening Post*:

> The school corridor rings with laughter, shaking the foil doilies that adorn posters and decorations put up on the walls.
> A huge Christmas tree, twice as tall as most of the youngsters, stands in the reception, decorated with baubles and tinsel.
> It is easy to feel the infectious excitement of the pupils of St Matthew's CE Primary School as Christmas draws near.

It is indeed.

THE WS

To be informative, interesting and – even – entertaining, a feature must answer all the Ws of a news story – that is, the who, what, when, where, why and how?

QUOTES

As in news stories, quotes lift the piece, substantiate and add to the facts, explain and bring human interest and insights, colour, drama and, occasionally, humour. David Bocking, for instance, a feature writer with the *Sheffield Telegraph*, gingered up a potentially uninspiring feature on a Scouts gang show with a number of apt and amusing quotes. The show, which involved a cast of 108, aged from 6 to their mid-70s, was a mix of comedy, music and dance, requiring a number of the young performers to don dresses, wigs and lacy blouses. Bocking used a quote from the show's director Andrew Watson to give a sense of the atmosphere pervading rehearsals:

'Most of them have to dress up and some have been fighting for the best dress,' says Andrew Watson. 'I've just heard one saying "I want that one because it goes with my pink blouse". They take it all very well.'

Quotes are also useful for changing pace and direction. Again, a quote from Bocking's piece illustrates the point:

One or two of the boys will be recreating the work of Tommy Cooper. 'He was an old magician who was quite funny and he sweated a lot,' explains 13-year-old Kevin Kerry. The Scouts are learning quite a bit from the experience clearly. 'Actually, this is one of the aims of the whole exercise,' says Andrew Watson, who enumerates a host of learning objectives hidden away behind the opportunities for cross-dressing.

In general, an interviewee in a feature will be quoted more extensively than in a news story, and individual quotes will be longer. In addition, particularly in a hard news feature or in an authoritative profile, more than one source will be quoted.

It goes without saying, of course, that quotes must be accurate and selected appropriately.

Lynn Barber (in Glover 2000: 201–2) stresses the importance of accuracy:

How accurate should quotations be? In my view, entirely accurate, dud grammar and all. Part of the joy of interviews is to reproduce different modes of speech, different turns of phrase, new words, new jargon, new extravagances of psychobabble. I am sometimes told off for using too many quotes, but surely it is mad to interview someone and not quote them? And I like the quotes to be exact, not some gentrified paraphrase. The only way in which I will tidy up a quote is to cut out excessive repetition of stock phrases like 'Do you know what I mean?' People who say 'Do you know what I mean?' tend to say it in every single sentence and it is just too painful to read over and over again. Nevertheless, I would always keep enough of them in to convey their frequent presence, and their irritation.

RESEARCH

Journalists will probably spend more time researching the subject for a feature than a news story and could find that they have too much information. The skill lies in selecting what is appropriate, interesting and relevant to the piece. Facts that are included must be accurate and sourced.

Facts that do not bring anything interesting to the feature, or cause an unnecessary diversion, should be jettisoned.

EFFECTIVE ENDINGS

An effective ending to a feature is one that reaches a conclusion, wraps the whole piece up or refers, in some way, to something referred to right at the start. Bocking's gang show piece provides a good example of this. His intro reads:

> There are times when it pays to have a very loud voice.
>   'Tuck your shirt in, Flynn,' bellows Andrew Watson. 'Matthew, pull your socks up, we can see everything.'

Bocking's last two pars, cleverly, refer back not only to the intro but also to the learning objectives outlined in the body of the piece by Andrew Watson, as well as to an earlier mention of the gang show Sea Scout standard 'Riding Along on the Crest of a Wave'. They read:

> No one appears to be scratching or picking anything they shouldn't but the grown-ups are misbehaving. 'Can the leaders please sit down,' Andrew bellows. The wave hasn't quite broken yet but in a few more days, and with a little more vocal encouragement, the Gang will surely be riding along on the crest of a whole new raft of life skill achievements.

LENGTH

Having said that the average newspaper feature is between 700 and 1000 words, always ask how many words are needed – and stick to the length given. Do not think that the feature length should reflect the time you have spent researching and writing it because, as Debbie Hall says: 'It'll only end up being cut to the length that was required in the first place.' Instead, learn to spot the important bits of research and interview that you can successfully use, and jettison the rest.

WRITE IT UP

There is a temptation among some writers to consolidate the information that they have found and delay the writing of a feature. Good advice would be to write up your copy as soon as possible after doing your interviews. Because of the nature of a feature, you will have more information than you need and the longer you delay, the more confusing that information will look.

CATEGORISE THIS ...

There are many different categories of features. There are those journalists who say features are anything in a newspaper that is neither news nor sport – and that includes everything from articles on local raves to restaurant reviews and from horoscopes to fashion tips. While we would not entirely agree that a recipe for a pudding containing whatever fruit happens to be in season is a feature in the classic understanding of the term, it would certainly appear on the features pages, or lifestyle pages as they are sometimes known.

NEWS BACKGROUNDER

News backgrounders are important features in that they offer more background and detail on people or events in the news. While a newspaper might carry a hard news story about a particular event on its front page, a backgrounder of about 700 words on an inside page offers further insight and explanation.

A backgrounder should contain added information and consider repercussions – how the situation or event has affected or will affect people, what are the causes and effects? A backgrounder might also consider other linked or similar events. For instance, a front-page lead in the *Sheffield Telegraph* about a takeover row between Dave Allen, chairman of Sheffield Wednesday football club, and former Chelsea boss Ken Bates, is accompanied on an inside page by a background feature by a specialist writer speculating and commenting on the origins of the row and what it means for the future security of the club.

COLOUR PIECE

As well as a news backgrounder, you might be asked to write a colour piece to go with a main news story. A colour piece would typically look behind the scenes of an event for something unusual or entertaining. For instance, in the case of a royal visit to the region, a colour piece would consider what their majesties were wearing, how many corgis were present and how many cars were in the regal motorcade.

FOLLOW-UP FEATURE

Like a backgrounder or colour piece, the follow-up feature follows a main news story, although not necessarily on the same day. For instance, a newspaper might run a news story about a child who has undergone life-saving medical treatment and follow it up a few days later with a more in-depth feature based on a longer interview with the child's parents.

LEADER PAGE FEATURE

Some newspapers go further than a news backgrounder and publish a leader page feature that analyses, comments on and delves deeper into the important news story of the day. (The leader page of a newspaper is important in that it carries the leaders or editorials – those columns made up of two or three individual comment pieces that reflect the newspaper's own opinions on the news stories of the day. These leaders or editorials are written by either the newspaper's own editor or its leader writers. It is unlikely that a junior reporter would be asked to write them.)

Leader page features are written by newspaper staff or by a guest writer, such as someone with specific, expert knowledge on the subject. (Look out for these people. A 'blob' at the end of the feature will often give details about the writer which can be logged in your contacts book for future reference.)

PERSONALITY, CELEBRITY OR CHARACTER PROFILES

Feature writing gives you the chance to meet personalities, celebrities and characters generally not available to the general public. They include film and music stars, authors, politicians and experts from the world of science and medicine working on major breakthroughs.

The point to remember is that, in meeting them, you are only getting a snapshot – you don't have time to get to know them and they are often only doing the interview to get publicity for their latest book, play, film or breakthrough.

Remember that the personality is probably on a book, play or film tour – they are doing the rounds and visiting as many different towns and cities as possible and being interviewed by many and various reporters. Chances are that they are saying the same things to every journalist they meet. Be aware of this and see if you can come up with a new, different or more interesting angle.

Be aware also of the public relations officer or publicist who sits in on the interview, takes over and tries to prevent you from asking certain questions.

OH, BUT I'M NOT FAMOUS ...

It is not always the famous personalities who make for the best features. Colleagues say that the most interesting characters they have written about have been ordinary people who have done extraordinary things. These characters include:

- the girl from Huddersfield fighting back after a stroke at the age of 22 to become a model
- the little nine-year-old girl from Swansea who saved her younger brother in a house fire and was so badly burnt herself that she is scarred for life
- the team of people planning to paraglide off Mount Everest
- the young mum, dying of cancer, who ran from John O'Groats to Land's End to raise money for charity.

Often such features are presented via the framework of a dramatic scenario or what Australian communications lecturer John Langer (2000: 117–18) describes as a 'strategic operation' that constructs a 'good victim' with whom the reader can identify: 'Victim stories work around some notion of consensus, but in this case one which is orientated towards the most ordinary routines of everyday life ... Mundane routines are established, only to be disrupted ... the normal course of events is fractured by a disruption seemingly outside any individual or community control.'

The aim is to encourage readers to identify with the victim and their powerlessness in the face of extraordinary and overwhelming circumstances. Says freelance journalist Carole Richardson: 'To an extent you have to build up a scenario – have a crisis at the start and then build it chronologically with lots of twists and turns, saving something surprising for the end. I found it quite difficult at first, but it comes naturally now and I would find it hard to write in any other way.'

It is a genre that is popular with readers, but one that requires sensitive handling on the part of the reporter if the interviewee is not to feel exploited. This is particularly an issue for Richardson, who is often required to write in the first person. In such cases, she always prefers to check back with her source: 'I never used to do this with newspapers, but with a lot of feature interviews I like to read stuff back to them. Nine times out of ten, it's OK and it's not a problem, but I feel that I need to check.'

SPECIALIST FEATURES

Specialist features are those that concentrate on specialist subjects, such as health, education, science, local government, the environment or business. They are usually written by a specialist correspondent, but general reporters will also have to write them from time to time.

GENERAL TOPICS

The topics that make for interesting features are many and various. The subjects below are just a small sample of features written recently by a Yorkshire-based freelance feature writer.

- The Barbie Dolls Collectors' Club – a woman from Ripon in North Yorkshire who has a collection of over 100 Barbie dolls in a display case at home. Did you know that a mint condition 1959 Barbie is worth anything up to £5000?
- The social niceties of air kissing when you meet friends – whether to make contact with just one cheek or both and the noises you should or shouldn't make.
- The Chocolate Society – a Yorkshire-based company that specialises in the real stuff, rather than over-the-counter brands.
- Making mousetraps – about a company in South Wales that manufactures mousetraps.
- One of the smallest theatres in the country – the Pateley Bridge Playhouse in North Yorkshire, which seats just 70 people.
- The latest tourist attraction – a Teesside cemetery and crematorium that was opening up to the public.
- Wine tasting – a doctor in Harrogate who formed a wine-tasting club on the basis that one or two glasses a day is good for you.
- Have Steinway will travel – a larger-than-life Yorkshire pianist (he is 6 feet 6 inches and 19 stone) who plays his Steinway in unusual places around the world. He's hired Carnegie Hall and Sydney Opera House, which is all well and good, but he's also transported his grand across deserts, down gorges, across rivers and had it lowered into place by helicopter to play at the Red Rose City at Petra, on the edge of the Grand Canyon, in a hot air balloon, and on platform one at Bingley railway station.

I'M GOING TRAVELLING

One of the perks of being a journalist is the number of free tickets that are sent for review purposes. Some journalists refuse to accept these, on the grounds that they are sent by organisations intent on receiving free and, hopefully, good publicity. However, in an industry where the pay of local and regional journalists is shamefully low and the perks pitifully few, the acceptance of free tickets – where appropriate and unsolicited – can be seen as an opportunity for good copy.

The unfortunate receive little more than a couple of tickets to listen to a little heard-of band playing in a remote village hall. However, there are dozens of other newspapers that are offered free flights and holidays in exotic destinations. As with all freebies, the journalist should not feel obliged to write anything other than the truth.

Used well by accredited journalists, tickets for free flights and holidays can lead to informative and entertaining features that highlight and expose destinations, warts and all.

There is also the opportunity to turn your own paid-for holidays into features. One colleague always looks for the opportunity to write about her annual trips. In the last few years she has taken holidays in:

- America – where she wrote a fashion feature about American business-women (they wore trainers to work – with their fur coats – because of the distances they had to walk from the subways to their offices and they put their high heels on once they had reached their desks)
- France – where she wrote about hiring bikes and cycling through remote villages, having forgotten it was Tour de France time
- India – where she met government ministers and wrote about the political situation in Delhi
- Nice – where she wrote about both camping and cuisine in the region.

REVIEWS

It is standard practice for regional and local papers to receive free tickets for press nights at local theatres and concert halls for the purpose of writing a review about the latest opera, concert, play or musical gig. In the same way, music companies and book publishers will send newly produced CDs and books to be reviewed.

The same rules apply that should be followed with all freebies: be honest in your appraisal.

The same rules apply in writing up a review that exist with any other type of story: it should be well written, have an intro that grabs the attention, be informative and/or entertaining, all the facts should be correct, the names of the various personalities involved, such as performer, producer, director, author, should be spelt correctly and any quotes used should be accurate.

Conventional wisdom has it that the past tense should be used for reviews where the event has happened and is not likely to be repeated, such as a one-off concert, but the present tense can be used where the review is of an ongoing performance, such as a play with a two-week run or a film.

While reviewing a performance or a book, make notes as you go along. If this is difficult – say, in the case of a darkened or crowded theatre or cinema – write down your thoughts and reactions as soon as possible once the event is over.

In a review, avoid giving away the whole story of the play, film or book. It is tempting – especially for someone new to reviewing – to simply retell the story. What is needed, however, is a flavour or synopsis.

Say what you liked or disliked about the item or event being reviewed and explain why, but be aware that the critical approaches towards an amateur production involving local schoolchildren, for instance, will not be the same as those used towards the latest Hollywood blockbuster. If you are going to criticise during a review, be sure that you can justify your censure and make sure you do not libel anyone. Remember, criticise the performance or the *product*, not the performer or the *producer*.

In the case of a play, film or book, you will need to decide whether or not to give away the ending. By doing so, you could spoil the enjoyment of someone thinking of going to see the play or film or reading the book. On the other hand, your readers will include those who have no intention of doing so and might appreciate knowing how it all ends. Experience shows that most reviewers suggest a twist or surprising denouement – if that is the case – but don't reveal exactly what it is.

THIS IS WHAT I THINK ...

The features section of a newspaper will often include the first person 'think' or reaction piece, which often carries a bylined picture of the writer and comes under such headings as 'I say ...', 'Think on ...', 'My word ...' or (worst of all) 'A sideways look at life ...'.

The best of these are written by well-informed writers, with strong and well-argued opinions, who talk *to* their readers, not *at* them. The worst are written by guest writers, who might include minor celebrities, such as a 'name' from the local TV or radio station. It could be suggested that the over-opinionated, knee-jerk reactionary views of a C-list celebrity wittering on about something that has little or no interest to the rest of us has had its day. We can but hope.

Experienced journalists are also filled with gloom when a valuable space such as this is used by a writer intent only on exposing and promoting the eccentricities of their own lives in the 'I'm daft, me …' school of self-indulgence.

A reporter given the chance of writing an 'I say …' column should see it as an opportunity to air strong, positive arguments that resonate with the reader or else certainly give them something to think about.

WATCH ME WHILE I …

Features much loved by young reporters are those in which the writer is put in situations where they can test their mettle and show off. Give them a stunt or a challenge and they will produce 900 words on the subject, plus pictures, faster than you can say, 'Take care – you could get hurt, be terri-fied or embarrassed.'

'Watch me …' features include reporters recounting their experiences of doing activities such as:

- bungee jumping
- parachuting
- driving at 100 mph on a skid pan
- paragliding in the Brecon Beacons
- learning to ski
- white water rafting
- going on an Army assault course.

The gentler variety include:

- finding your inner child in a flotation tank
- having facials, massages and other treatments in the name of 'women's interest'
- testing spas, champagne, stretch limousines
- spending the day with a personal shopper
- going back to your old school for the day.

The opportunity to try out new experiences is, for many feature writers, one of the best things about the job. For instance, Debbie Hall is still enthusiastic about the day that she stuck her head into a magician's guillotine:

I suppose I'm one of very few people who have had their heads chopped off and lived to tell the tale. I inspected the equipment and watched the blade cut two carrots in half, but I still don't know how it was done or why my head is still on my shoulders.

I've done a parachute drop, too, and once I flew in a flight simulator – I crashed just off the ring road in Bradford for anybody who is interested.'

ADVERTORIALS

Journalists are increasingly asked to write advertorials, which are articles written in the style of an editorial but paid for by the advertiser. They are usually marked as 'Advertising' or 'Special feature' when they appear in the newspaper, but, otherwise, there is little to differentiate them from other feature articles. Subjects range from tile warehouses and garden centres to kitchen and conservatory showrooms, from recruitment agencies and office furniture outlets to fashion boutiques and Rolls-Royce suppliers.

The fact that the feature is being paid for should not tempt you to write eulogies. You should be objective, honest and accurate, and approach it as you would any other news story – that is, look for the best angle, intro and line.

This is one area where a journalist's copy is sent to the originator for approval on the basis that the originator – the advertiser – is paying for the feature. However, to let anyone outside the newspaper see your copy before it goes to print goes totally against the grain.

FACT BOX

Not only will a fact box break up a page of print, but a journalist can use it to offer at-a-glance information and statistics that either do not sit easily or would be lost in the body of the text. For instance, a feature on a child patient in a local hospice could include a fact box with contact details, the main historical dates of the hospice movement, locations of other hospices and the number of families benefiting from hospice care.

STYLES

Q: WHEN SHOULD I USE A Q&A STYLE?
A: WHEN IT'S APPROPRIATE.

The Q&A style of feature writing, where the journalist's questions are marked with a Q, given in full and highlighted in bold, and the interviewee's answers are marked with an A and are also given in full, serve the purpose of recounting faithfully the entire conversation, leaving the reader in no doubt about what was said. This style of feature offers no comment or analysis, observation or colour other than what the reader can glean from the questions and answers themselves.

If you have no definite angle in mind when you set out to do a particular interview or you know the interviewee will have a lot of important things to say on a variety of different subjects, a Q&A style might suit you best. However, it would still be advisable to edit the piece where appropriate as not all that is said will be of interest.

I AM INVOLVED

The first person style of feature is one in which the writer makes reference to him- or herself in the piece. They make reference, for instance, to how they felt on the day of the interview, how they reached the location of the interview, what the interviewee was wearing and what his or her demeanour was. There may even be reference to whether the interviewee was hot, bothered, late, cross or about to burst into tears.

These first person features contain a lot of observations and will only be appropriate in certain types of feature. This would be the case, for instance, where the character and behaviour of the interviewee is all-important or where the writer is a known name or local celebrity and considers him- or herself to be as important as the interviewee.

ARE YOU FAMILIAR WITH THIS?

A style that suggests familiarity between the writer and the reader is commonly used on newspaper lifestyle and women's pages. The feature suggests a knowing and joint interest in the subjects written about. Features of this sort commonly address the reader as 'you' or, in the case of women's pages, 'girls like us ...'.

WRITING FEATURES: THE RECIPE

As with news stories, features are essentially about people, and even a serious subject, such as health service reforms, requires a human dimension. Remember, the intro should act as a teaser and taster, so, particularly in a feature, it is not necessary to give the whole game away at once.

Debbie Hall, writing in the January 2004 edition of *The Journal*, a monthly magazine produced by Hull Daily Mail Publications, does this as she begins her goats' cheese-making feature:

> It's one long round of changing nappies, feeds and general nurturing for an East Riding couple.

The word picture she paints is one with which most parents would identify and suggests, without her actually spelling it out, the mind-blowing drudgery as well as the emotional rewards of parenthood.

The next par provides the context:

> Nothing so special in that, you might think, but the 'charges' in Tom and Tricia Wallis's care are actually cheeses, and a herd of 30 adult goats and 20 kids which support the dairy business they run.

She begins by emphasising the normality of the situation she outlines and then provides both context and contrast by identifying the nature of the Wallis's business and the size of their herd. Nothing so normal about that, after all.

The following pars make it clear what the feature is about:

> Tom and Tricia's Lowna Dairy is a small but busy affair, based on the same site at Raywell, near Cottingham, as their thriving kennels and cattery.
>
> But word about Lowna, and its products, is spreading all the time and the Wallises are becoming known as the 'big cheeses' in the rural community after achieving epicurean notoriety at a number of top shows.
>
> The couple, describing themselves as 'a plain and simple man and woman, enjoying the simple life and good food', were suddenly thrust into the limelight this year by a cheese named Rowley Round. The white, fresh goats' cheese, produced at their smallholding, was responsible for bringing home a silver medal at the British Cheese Awards at Blenheim Palace.

The first par establishes the location. The second tells the reader why the couple are in the news and the third details the precise nature of their achievements. Note the use of the words 'epicurean notoriety'. Epicurean suggests a touch of class – these are not amateurs, mucking about with a bit of curds and whey, but professionals, producing a premier product. Notoriety, on the other hand, implies that people are talking about them – they have achieved a degree of fame in their particular world. The mention, too, of Blenheim Palace adds a touch of glamour and grandeur – clearly the British Cheese Awards are no Mickey Mouse affair.

Having established the scenario and provided a context, the main body copy provides more information about the cheese-making successes of the Wallises, adds detail about the products they make (not too much – this is a human interest feature, not an advertorial) and outlines some of the work involved in keeping goats and producing cheese. Here, an explanation is provided of the 'nappy changing' activities mentioned in the intro.

Finally, the concluding pars return to the notion of the pair as a plain and simple man and woman with a quote from Tom Wallis:

> 'This is just something Tricia and I are passionate about. We are only very small, but we are aiming to do it right and be there for people,' said Tom.
> 'It's just pleasant living here on this hillside, out in the country, and enjoying what we do.'
> Clearly a simple couple enjoying the good life.

Exercise

Get a copy of a local weekly or evening newspaper and identify three news stories that could be developed into a feature.

Also, look through the classified ads pages and identify three advertisements that could be followed up and developed as features.

SOURCES AND CONTACTS BOOKS

'... there isn't any news,' said Ginger. 'My father's always sayin' there isn't any news. Whenever my mother asks him at breakfast what news there is in the paper he always says there isn't any.'

'Well, we can invent news can't we?' said William. 'I bet that's what real ones do, invent it if there isn't any ...'

R. Crompton, *William and the Space Animal* (1992: 110)

This chapter:

- examines what sources are
- considers where journalists get their news and information
- looks at who the essential contacts are
- shows how to set up a contacts book so that it is most effective and efficient.

Regional newspaper editor David Ward cherishes the advice that he was offered by his first boss, who, early in Ward's career, took him to one side and told him to get himself off to the pub.

No, young Ward was not being given carte blanche to get drunk on company time. (Nor are we suggesting that you should do so either.) Instead, Ward's editor was offering him a valuable tip on where to find news stories and ideas. Despite what Richmal Crompton's young scally-wag William Brown suggests above, journalists *do not* invent stories.

Put simply, a story would not be a story without a source. That sounds obvious, but it bears saying anyway because one of the questions a journalist is most frequently asked is: 'Where do you get your stories?' The answer is, invariably: 'My sources.'

Where do you find sources? That's easy. Sources are everywhere – pulling a pint at the pub, scanning goods at the supermarket checkout, chatting at the school gate, punching tickets on the bus ... sources are wherever you find people. That was the point that David's editor – a dyed-in-the-wool Yorkshireman – was making.

Ward, now editor of the *Pontefract and Castleford Express*, says:

> It's important to be known. I get more feedback and tip-offs from being known in three or four pubs around town than from almost any other single source.
>
> It's advice I was given on my very first day – to get myself known to a few pub landlords and their customers – and, 30 years later, that's what I still tell trainees. You have to look at the community you're in. If I go into a pub in Castleford and sit drinking a Coke and try to get information out of people, they'll feel as if I'm using them, but if I sit here with a couple of beers and chat to the lads and whoever is in, I'm one of them. Someone they can trust.

Ward raises a number of important issues here – not least that sourcing news is a bit more complicated than simply nursing a pint at the local. People are rightly wary of reporters who appear to be lurking in the hope of snaffling a scoop. However, he also touches on the important point that successful journalists are embedded in the communities in which they report. This is true to a greater or lesser extent at every level of journalism and is both a good thing and a bad thing, too.

WHAT DO YOU MEAN, EMBEDDED?

Embedded is a trendy term that first cropped up in 2003 during the second Gulf war when journalists advanced into Iraq alongside the US and UK armed forces. These journalists were said to be embedded with the troops and, because of their unique frontline position, were able to provide vivid pictures of the conflict as it unfolded. As *The Observer*'s columnist Peter Preston observed, people back home were able to ride into battle with the marines. It was exciting stuff.

On the other hand, the fate of the embedded correspondents was tied so closely to that of their military protectors that, inevitably, there were accusations that their reportage was tainted by a conflict of interests. It is hard, after all, not to empathise with the perspective of the men on the front line when you have smelled their sweat and shared their dug-out latrines.

This is only natural. Journalism is about empathy – about seeing the world through someone else's eyes and reflecting that view to a wider community – and empathising with a particular viewpoint automatically impede one's impartiality. However, in the desert the facts being fed to the embeds could not always be indep verified by other than military sources. Essentially, for the embedded correspondents, there proved to be 'a great difference between being in a position to give coverage to a source organisation's event, process or state of affairs and having access that allows for the story the journalist needs for his news organisation's purposes' (Ericson et al. in Tumber 1999: 280). Getting too close to a source can mean giving too much credence to his or her view of events, thus compromising your ability to report the wider picture. The unique position of the embeds meant that the news they reported represented only one perspective – that of the military and the politicians who sent them to war.

This, in a nutshell, strikes at the heart of the problem with all sources of news – the question of agenda and the extent to which the agenda of a journalist, embedded within a particular community, coincides with that of his or her sources.

THE JOURNALISTIC AGENDA

The journalistic agenda, as we have already made clear, is to report the news objectively and impartially – a Herculean task as it requires a separation from self that is almost impossible to achieve. In fact, there are 'a variety of potential journalistic accounts of events, corresponding to the plurality of viewpoints which exist in the world. More than one of these accounts may have validity' (McNair 2001: 36). Inevitably, how we see the world is formed by the ideas, influences and events that have shaped us. Significantly, however, the journalist's view of the world is also coloured by the information presented by his or her sources. Essentially, 'sources cooperate with reporters to the extent that their sources believe they and/or their ideas will gain favourable public access' (McManus in Tumber 1999: 186). Accordingly, the military (and their political masters) welcomed the embeds in Iraq because they provided a conduit through which they could transmit a positive spin on their conduct of the war. After all, 'positively framed coverage beats neutral or critical reporting' (McManus in Tumber 1999: 187). Certainly, reports of the brave advance of the allies and their warm reception by the local population, were instrumental in persuading the home audience that the UK's involvement in the war was justified.

On one level, therefore, it could be argued that the embeds (and the employers who consented to their deployment) were grossly naïve in allowing themselves to be so skilfully manipulated – except, of course, that naïvety is not normally a trait associated with journalism. Therefore, while the news organisations that deployed the embedded correspondents were certainly guilty of using them to obtain information at the least cost, (McManus in Tumber 1999: 187), most were also astute enough to have other men and women elsewhere in the field to provide an alternative viewpoint to what Peter Preston described as the 'slices of war' served up by the embeds. Moreover, quoted in *The Guardian*, Richard Sambrook, the BBC's director of news, made it clear that access to alternative sources of information was crucial to transparent reportage of the war: 'Reporting the war is about putting together fragments of information. We're all trying to work out this jigsaw and what the overall picture is.'

The jigsaw metaphor is a good one. Writing news is about sourcing sometimes disparate pieces of information and bringing them together to make a coherent whole. Put simply, sources provide facts and, the more facts a journalist has at his or her disposal, the more rounded and complete the final picture. Put even more simply, never rely on just one source of information – always check your facts and, when you have done that, check them again.

SO, WHERE DO YOU GET YOUR STORIES?

Look at any news story and consider where it might come from. Here are some examples.

- The main source for the story headlined: **POLICE APPEAL FOR WITNESSES TO FATAL ROAD CRASH,** would be the police.
- Information about this: **MUM PRAISES HERO WHO SAVED HER SON IN HOUSE BLAZE,** would have been given by the fire brigade, who told us about the fire, and the mum, who told us about her son's rescuer.
- The source for this headline: **POSTMAN TO GIVE UP ROUND AFTER LOTTERY WIN,** could come from the Lottery organiser and the postman himself.

SOURCING YOUR STORY

The sources identified above can be divided into two distinct groups:

- on-diary sources
- off-diary sources.

Broadly speaking, off-diary sources are those that produce unexpected, and unanticipated, news stories – the press release in the post providing information about a company's million pound overseas contract, newspaper and billboard advertisements featuring the new face of the Countryside Alliance and, in a local paper, the obituary notice that announces the death of a retired headteacher or other figure once prominent in the community.

Diary sources are rather more predictable and fall into two categories:

- those sources reporters contact regularly as a matter of routine (for instance, the police, fire brigade, schools and community groups, plus authority figures such as councillors, business leaders and local church people)
- those contacted to provide information about an event or happening listed in the office diary.

Such listings include a mix of regular events, such as the monthly meeting of the local council, as well as one-off specials. For example, a note in the diary about a music festival will prompt the news editor to assign a reporter to contact the organiser, probably a week or two beforehand, for a pre-event trail and, afterwards, for a post-event write-up.

Clearly, there is some overlap between these two sources. Some journalists, for instance, would list the emergency services as off-diary sources, as gruesome murders, house blazes and motorway pile-ups are, by their nature, unexpected and unanticipated. However, we put them firmly into the diary category as police, fire and ambulance personnel are all people who will be contacted on a regular and predictable basis.

THE MOST COMMON SOURCES OF NEWS

DIARY
- Emergency services – fire, police and ambulance.
- Churches, mosques, synagogues and so on – both places of worship and national bodies, such as the General Synod.
- Councils – including parish, town, district and county.
- Courts – including magistrates', crown, coroners' and county.
- Newsroom diary – which may list local galas, cheque presentations, school sports days, amateur dramatic performances, university graduations, meetings of local organisations, businesses and groups.
- Press conferences.
- Public inquiries and other public meetings, such as employment tribunals.
- Reports from public bodies or other organisations, such as Ofsted.
- Schools – primary and secondary.

- Sixth-form and further education colleges.
- Universities and higher education institutions.

OFF-DIARY

- Adverts – those that appear in your newspaper and elsewhere, such as billboards, posters and so on.
- Cuttings – from your own newspaper and others.
- Experts – for instance, specialists in their own field.
- Media – including other journalists, newspapers, TV and radio, trade press, internal communications and corporate publications, as well as specialist journals.
- Members of the public – including gossip and titbits you happen to overhear.
- Noticeboards – including those in the post office or newsagents, outside churches or on walls of businesses.
- Political parties.
- News agencies.
- Newspaper library.
- Press officers.
- Press releases.
- Readers' letters.
- Victims.
- Whistleblowers.
- Witnesses.

SOURCES THAT YOU WILL USE REGULARLY

Some of these sources – such as the police, fire and ambulance services – are more important than others and journalists are in regular contact with them. Most newsrooms make frequent calls to the emergency services throughout the day to check if anything is happening or to get an update on an earlier or ongoing incident.

Press releases are another important source and, although they arrive by the hundreds in newspaper offices – by post, fax and e-mail – they are ignored at the journalist's peril. Often they herald a forthcoming press conference or event, which is then logged in the newsroom diary. Often, too, the press release has been either deliberately or innocently written so that the newsworthy value of the release is buried in the 'Note to Eds' section at the end.

The media feeds off itself and often journalists trawl the rest of the media for stories (apart from anything else, it is important for journalism students and trainee journalists to keep an eye on what the rest of the media is doing, how and why). So, cuttings are important – both those culled from today's newspapers and those logged electronically on a database.

It is worth looking at the letters page of your paper. Buried among the opinions and comments of Mr Harumpher of Hull and Miss Misery of Margate is often a story gem. Look in the small ads, too – someone might just be selling a rare, lesser-spotted African parrot, the only one of its kind in the UK, which could make a good picture story.

Identify and cultivate experts. These will include university lecturers who are specialists in their own field and could give an authoritative comment and/or background to a story you are writing. Likewise, doctors, especially those who specialise in particular areas of medicine.

Also, of course, you cannot forget members of the public. These include your readers who phone or write in, people who come into the newspaper's front office to talk to you, relatives, friends and colleagues who tell you things, people you overhear on a bus and strangers you strike up a conversation with in the pub, on the street or any time while out and about.

The best sources are people – someone, somewhere knows someone who knows something that you want to know more about. Just as in any other relationship, trust, respect and consideration are the bedrocks on which the relationship between journalist and source must be founded. Forget this at your peril, says David Ward:

> There's a suspicion about journalists that we're only interested in using people to get stories. To an extent, that's true but you have to have integrity as well. If someone tells me something off the record, it stays off the record, and if they ask me not to use something they've told me, I won't. I might explain to them why I think what they've told me is worth a story, but, if they still say 'no' I'm not going to spoil the relationship by using something they want to keep confidential.
>
> You've got to think long-term – by betraying somebody now, I might get this one story, but I'll lose all the other equally good stories that might come from that source.
>
> The good thing is that, because people know me and know that they can trust me, they will often give me the go-ahead.

Ward is infuriated, though, by national journalists, from both print and broadcast media, who jeopardise that trust:

> People like me, reporters and editors on weekly newspapers, put a lot of work into gaining the trust of our readers, but, as soon as a big national story comes up, everybody else comes in and treads on everybody's feet and that gives us all a bad name. Then, they beggar off because the story has become last week's news and we have to spend the next six months rebuilding trust again because of the damage that has been caused.

PUT IT IN THE BOOK

A contacts book is one of the most valuable tools a journalist possesses – almost as important as a notebook and pen because, without it, the job would be much more difficult and take considerably longer.

A contacts book contains the names, numbers and details of valuable contacts and sources who will add authenticity, an authoritative voice, fact, detail and colour to a story. Without those names and numbers being readily available, journalists can waste time scratching their heads thinking of people to contact and thumbing through well-used telephone directories looking for numbers, which are sometimes out of date and are generally used only in office hours and therefore not much good if it is after 6 pm.

Journalists might turn to Web-based directories, which is all well and good, supposing that there is a full list of numbers – direct lines to office, home and mobile – and the numbers enable the journalist to reach the person when the journalist wants to reach them, but it all takes time. It is far better to have logged in your contacts book the personal and direct numbers and e-mail details for the contact you need rather than just the number of the organisation that the person works for as, then, you will find you have to talk your way past switchboard operators, personal assistants and deputies.

HAVE I GOT YOUR NUMBER?

Many colleagues have logged contact details since they started work as journalists. With every interviewee they meet, they ask for out-of-office-hours and home numbers and, more recently, also mobile phone numbers and e-mail details. This information can be vital. One colleague recalls how, when working a shift on a national tabloid, she was asked to contact a number of actors and, as it was the week before Christmas, ask them what type of Christmas cards they were sending (OK, corny, but it is a typical seasonal story). As luck would have it, over the years she had interviewed and profiled a fair number of actors as and when they had appeared at the theatre in the town where she worked or had agreed to do an interview to plug their new film or play. During each interview, she had asked for follow-up numbers 'just in case I need to contact you for anything else' and generally she had been given mobile numbers, a direct line to an agent or, in a surprising number of cases, home numbers. So, rather than having to waste time looking for these details, she already had a list of likely sources stored in her contacts book.

This colleague guards her book with her life, but, like many journalists, she is not above taking a crafty look in any colleagues' books left lying around.

Debbie Hall, a former court reporter for the *Hull Daily Mail*, made a point of keeping a record of the first names and surnames of all the barristers, solicitors and judges on her patch. All were recorded in what she calls her bible:

I've still got it and I still make a point of keeping lists. It makes life a lot easier. It's all very well asking someone their name the first time you see them in court, but if you have to ask them a second and third time – and, let's face it, it's easy to forget names – they soon get fed up. It makes you look inefficient and unprofessional, too.

WHAT TYPE OF BOOK?

Hardback, indexed books are the best. They are durable, classification is straightforward and, once entries have been entered alphabetically, they are quick and easy to use.

Colleagues who have relied on ring-binder-type books all make the same comment: that it is too easy to cram little bits of paper containing numbers in between the pages rather than log the information properly. It makes finding those numbers difficult and the tendency is for the scraps of paper to become torn, fall out and get lost.

Others who have used electronic organisers have discovered the efficacy of also keeping a hardback copy. Organisers that rely on battery power or electric charging can run out of steam, just when they are needed. Also, as one colleague found to his cost, when you have stored every valuable name and number in your electronic organiser, the years of collating them count for nothing when you spill coffee over it.

If you plan to use your PC to log names and numbers, do so, but make backup and hard copies, too. It is preferable to make your hard copy a book that you can carry around with you. Remember, when you are out on the road on a story, you will not have access to your PC, but the book in your pocket might just save the day.

SHOULD I STORE IT HERE?

What should you store in your contacts book? It should certainly contain full names of people and organisations – and that includes first and/or Christian names and surnames and the names of organisations, as they like to style themselves – main switchboard numbers, direct lines, mobile phone numbers, home numbers, fax numbers, out-of-hours numbers (if different from home numbers), e-mail addresses and, sometimes, home addresses.

ESSENTIALS

Among the essential numbers that you should have in your contacts book are the following.

LOCAL NUMBERS FOR ...

- Airports.
- Big-name organisations the head offices of which are based in your area or have the name of your area in the title. For instance, local and regional journalists in Yorkshire would need to include organisations such as Yorkshire Water, Yorkshire Bank, Yorkshire Electricity and so on.
- Bus and rail companies and stations.
- Churches and other places of worship.
- Community groups, including ethnic minority, gay and lesbian groups and local pressure groups.
- Councils, councillors and MPs.
- Courts, including coroners' courts.
- Coastguards, if near the sea.
- Emergency services – police, fire and ambulance, including press office numbers.
- Environmental agency.
- Government departments based regionally.
- Hospitals, health authorities and trusts.
- Media organisations – including other newspapers, TV and radio stations.
- Prisons.
- Schools, sixth-form colleges and further education colleges and universities.
- Sports grounds and leisure centres.
- Theatres.
- Tourist attractions.
- Trade unions, chambers of commerce and industry.

NATIONAL NUMBERS FOR ...

- Automobile Association (AA).
- Church of England.
- Confederation of British Industry (CBI).
- Government departments.
- House of Commons.
- National media.
- Royal Automobile Club (RAC).
- Services – Royal Navy, Royal Air Force and Army.
- Trades Union Congress (TUC).

PEOPLE CONTACTS

List people under their job/interest rather than their name if they are not well known as you might forget the name while remembering what they do or did, but cross-reference them if necessary.

Under people contacts you could list the following.

- Academics – especially those who can speak on specialist subjects.
- Actors.
- Artists.
- Astrologers.
- Astronomers.
- Authors.
- Businesspeople.
- Celebrities.
- Councillors.
- Doctors – especially those working in specialist medical areas.
- Financial experts – for instance, for budget stories.
- Media pundits.
- Solicitors.
- Teachers.
- Vicars and other ministers of religion and faith leaders – especially outspoken clerics.
- Victims – for instance, children who have triumphed over tragedy.

GENERAL

You can never be sure when you will need general numbers, such as the following but you will need them at some time.

- Action, campaign and pressure groups.
- Buckingham Palace.
- *Burke's Peerage.*
- Charities.
- Cinemas and theatres.
- Civic Trust.
- Collectors' clubs.
- Community groups.
- Conference centres.
- Farmers and farming organisations.
- Jobcentres.
- Libraries.
- Museums and art galleries.

(Continued)

(Continued)

- National Trust.
- NCP.
- Neighbourhood Watch.
- NSPCC.
- Parks.
- Political parties.
- Post offices.
- Prisons.
- Pubs and restaurants.
- Retailers.
- RSPCA.
- TV soap press officers.
- Youth organisations.

THE CLOSER THE BETTER

Where possible always try to source information from the person closest to the story. This is not always possible, especially for stories involving large organisations or institutions. Sadly, the duty sergeant at the local police station is unlikely to allow today's reporters to flick unattended through the front desk incident book and cherry pick the juiciest news, as a colleague recalls being allowed to do. David Ward blames the public relations industry:

> Sources of news have changed and a lot of it is to do with press officers. It used to be possible to ring up and speak to the head of housing, for instance, and he was authorised to give a comment. Now, reporters have to go through the press office and they come out with something extremely bland. Worse, if you've got an exclusive and ring them up for a comment, they fax the response to every other publication so it's no longer exclusive.

The solution is to develop proper relationships with the individuals involved. While they have a duty to present their organisations in the best possible light, most have some degree of flexibility with regard to how much or how little they can tell you. Reporters who have won the respect and liking of a press officer will be privileged to rather more information than those who treat them with disdain.

Recognise, too, that, just because the organisation wants you to source information exclusively from its press office, you are not duty bound to do so. If the head of housing, a paid employee of the council, cannot speak to you, ring the chair of the housing committee instead. He or she is an elected member of the council and, therefore, answerable to the electors, who are also your readers. If he or she is a bit reticent, phone the shadow chair or the maverick councillor who has no hope of promotion to the front bench and likes making waves.

RECIPROCITY OF INTEREST

As we've explored, both at the beginning of this chapter and elsewhere in the book, the whole issue of sourcing news is a thorny one. Theorists, in the main, see journalists as largely uncritical conduits propagating not news, but, rather, the dominant ideologies of those who control power and resources. Intellectually, it is hard to argue convincingly that this is not the case as journalists are, by virtue of their education, profession and income, part of the dominant oligarchy. Thus, journalists are 'drawn into a symbiotic relationship' with powerful sources 'by reciprocity of interest' (Herman and Chomsky in Tumber 1999: 172–3). In other words, it is not in the material interests of journalists to challenge the status quo. This is a message that a colleague remembers Greg Philo of the Glasgow Media Unit proffer during an Open University summer school debate more than two decades ago. At the time, young and idealistic, she was outraged that she and her kind should be perceived as establishment tools, but, latterly, her more world-weary self concedes that Philo might have had a point.

This is where the notion of gatekeeping comes in – by making decisions about what does and does not constitute news, newspaper people are opening and closing the news gate, giving access to some people and organisations and denying access to others. Inevitably, the tendency is to favour those who can provide a steady diet of facts and opinions, which, in turn, means that the news agenda is dominated by town halls, courts, the police, business and industry – all organisations that 'turn out a large volume of material that meets the demands of news organisations for reliable, scheduled flows' (Herman and Chomsky in Tumber 1999: 173).

Essentially, pressing deadlines encourage dependency and, consequently, news acquires what theorists describe as an ideological content. Journalism's function becomes not the dissemination of news but 'one of social reproduction in the service, not of society as a whole, but of its dominant groups and classes … the information media [become] producers of ideology, representing the interests of an elite minority to the subordinate majority' (McNair 2001: 22). This results in a sort of one-way traffic that involves ' "them" telling "us" what they want us to know', which the media, 'being, "objective" faithfully reproduces … even if it is a pack of lies or just plain daft' (Masterman 1994: 120–1).

In other words, the media acts as an uncritical conduit between those in power and authority and those whom they wish to control.

RAISED EYEBROWS

This is not a view of journalism that most journalists would recognise. Most would insist that how they source and write the news is entirely driven by readership needs and expectations and would be inclined to point to the huge numbers of column inches devoted to stories criticising council decisions and championing the rights of council taxpayers, for instance, as evidence of the willingness of journalists to challenge the status quo. Yet, there is a grain of truth in the media as conduit theory. Official sources, or those deemed politically or socially acceptable, are prioritised over less authoritative or non-politically correct sources. Just as history always tells the story of the victor, the one who dominates, so news tends to foreground the point of view of the dominant group in society, rather than that of the underdog. In *Journalism: Principles and practice*, Tony Harcup (2004: 68), a lecturer at the University of Sheffield, cites a story that he covered as a young reporter concerning complaints about a group of Gypsies: 'Eyebrows were raised in the newsroom when I said I was going to ask the Gypsies themselves for their version of events. It seemed that a comment from the police or local authority was thought to be sufficient to balance the story.' Nevertheless, he persisted and got a better story as a result as the Gypsies, fed up with being hounded from pillar to post, threatened to retaliate by moving their caravans into the centre of town. 'It was not rocket science,' observes Harcup, 'just good journalism, but it remains unusual to see Gypsies or asylum seekers quoted in response to allegations against them.'

A PRICE TO PAY

There is no doubt, says one colleague, that some sources – in particular, councillors and other authoritative community figures and opinion formers – do seek to mould coverage of events and issues to suit their own agendas. She cites the example of a prominent, sometimes controversial, local politician who, when a new junior joined the staff, made a big point of ringing the office to welcome her to the community. She must, says this colleague, have felt very flattered. A couple of days later, he approached her at a meeting and made a big fuss of her, introducing her to people and telling her to come to him if she needed anything. It was so obvious that he was being nice because he thought that he could use her as a mouthpiece and she would be too inexperienced to realise what was happening: 'I've become very cynical. People try to take you in all the time. It makes you very distrustful of people and their motives, but, I suppose, the very fact that I'm always thinking "Why are you telling me this?" means that I'm less likely to be duped.'

ANONYMOUS SOURCES

It is always possible that you will have a contact who is prepared to provide you with the information that you need, but prefers not to be publicly identified as a source. Two points here. First, if a source requests anonymity you are honour-bound to protect their confidence. This involves not only keeping their identity secret from readers and from everyone else in the office – with the possible exception of your editor – but also taking the necessary steps to ensure that others cannot trace the connection between you. The renowned Jean Morgan, who retired in 2003 after 19 years with the *Press Gazette*, was famous for her careful protection of sources and, according to a profile in the magazine, frequently used a pseudonym when ringing through to newsrooms so as not to compromise those she was calling.

Second, although your source may be more frank and open if he or she knows that any remarks will not be attributed directly, readers are, rightly, suspicious of unattributed quotes. As Chris Page, editor of the *Selby Times* observes, they cast doubt on the veracity of the story being reported:

> The only time we'll use anonymous quotes is if there is any possibility of a backlash against the source. For instance, if we were running a story about the neighbours from hell, we wouldn't identify the people who spoke out against them, but we would check and double-check the facts and the credibility of our source. And, if we were in any doubt at all, we wouldn't run the story.
>
> It's not enough for a story to be true. It is also important that it is believed and, unfortunately, an anonymous quote is on a par with 'no comment'. It speaks volumes.

Further, the more anonymous quotes are used, the more readers discount them, which, in turn, creates a barrier between reader and reporter. Put succinctly, naming names adds credibility.

Exercise

You are working for a local paper in Yorkshire. You are given the following news tips. Find the names and telephone numbers of contacts who could speak authoritatively about each of them. You need to explain how you found each name and number and why the contacts would be good sources.

1 Hoteliers in your town are up in arms about a plan by the local authority to stop putting their details in tourist information guides. The council claims that hoteliers have been giving false information about facilities and standards and, until an inquiry is carried out, are not including hotel details in its guides.
2 A well-known author has written a travel book looking at towns and villages around Britain. He is less than complimentary about your town, saying that it has little charm, no history to speak of, few leisure facilities and no decent restaurants.
3 A dog breeder in Essex has said that southern dogs are distinctly better bred than those in the north.
4 There is a rumour of a new EU ruling on chocolate. Apparently, the over-the-counter chocolate sold in Britain is not real chocolate and, therefore, can no longer be called chocolate.

(Answers are given at the end of the book.)

INTERVIEWING

'I hate talking about myself.'
   'I dare say, but you've got to when you're being interviewed.'

P. G. Wodehouse, *Bachelors Anonymous* (1975: 114)

This chapter:

- tells you the general rules of interviewing
- discusses where and how interviews should be conducted
- explains what the journalist needs to know and do in advance
- considers the research needed before an interview
- shows how to set up an interview
- explains how to take control
- looks at different types of interviews.

Journalism is about getting information and one of the best ways of doing this is by asking questions. Lots of them.

A journalist can use any number of research tools – from cuttings to reference books and from noticeboards to the Internet – and, in many background-type stories, this may be enough. However, to get all the information a journalist needs to make a story interesting and give it depth and/or colour, there is no better way than interviewing someone who knows about the subject and asking them questions (Bell 1991: 57):

> Journalistic wisdom holds that there is no substitute for talking to a newsmaker ... based on the (quite true) premise that the story narrated verbally is likely to be more focused, more simply expressed and offer the chance of more useable quotes than a written document.

The importance of interviews to good news stories cannot be overstated.

BE PREPARED

Most stories come from interviews of one kind or another – from a simple chat with a stranger to a lengthy session with the chief executive of a large corporation. Whoever the interviewee, preparation is vital. Some journalists have interviews thrust on them with little or no time to prepare – for instance, a member of the public arrives at the newspaper's front office and wants to speak to a reporter straight away. However, even in this situation, you need to ask the news desk before setting off: 'Who are they? What do they want?' Certainly, avoid going into an interview cold.

Some journalists say that they never prepare for an interview – they treat the process as a conversation and, having asked the first question, let nature take its course. They claim to pick up on the answers they are given, allowing for relaxed, conversational flow. This is all very well, but it could be argued that the journalist gets borne along and the interviewee is able to dictate the shape and tone of the interview. You could also get back to the newsroom and find that you do not have answers to some important questions because you did not ask them, or, worse, have had a nice chat, but not got the story.

THE PURPOSE OF THE INTERVIEW

All interviews take place for a reason – usually because someone, somewhere has an idea to sell, a film, book or product to launch or a crusade or cause to bring to people's attention. It is a good idea to be clear in your head before going into an interview just what the interviewee's motives might be – what is it that they want to tell you? Perhaps what is it that they do not want to tell you? It is important to remember that the reasons for an interviewee granting an interview may not necessarily coincide with your reasons for wanting to interview them. Put simply, you have different goals and expectations and these may not always be mutually compatible. As the late American media magnate William Randolph Hearst so succinctly observed: 'All news is something somebody wants suppressed. All the rest is advertising.' (Harris and Spark 1998: 5).

Broadly speaking, all interviewees have a story to tell (or sell), while interviewers have news pages to fill and, as a result, the two come together in what Fiammetta Rocco (in Glover 2000: 49), former UK Press Awards feature writer of the year, regards as a complicated ritual that can become a kind of co-dependence:

> The journalist needs the 'story', the closeness to the subject, the intimacy that will yield fresh insights. The subject, meanwhile, has needs of his own: above all to maintain the journalist's interest and stop him getting bored, and to persuade him or her that the subject's version of the story is the whole and only 'story'.

For the interviewee, the journalist is the means by which he or she presents his or her version of reality to a wider public, while, for the journalist, the interviewee or source allows him or her to present a wider picture of reality to the public.

RESEARCH

Before doing an interview, you need to do some research to learn something about the subject. Interviewees are generally impressed if you know something about them or what it is that they are involved in, but avoid pretending to know more than you do. Get the interviewee to repeat and explain wherever necessary. You could even apologise for your ignorance on certain matters and then go on to explain that this is why you are interviewing him or her – the expert.

As part of your research you could:

- look through the cuttings file in the newsroom library to see what has been written about the person or subject before
- check if he or she is in *Who's Who*
- check if there is anything about the subject in today's papers – for instance, your story might be a follow-up
- check if there is a press release about the subject or any agency copy available
- look at any other material that might have arrived – for instance, if a local author is plugging a new book, see if the book or dust jacket has been sent
- speak to your colleagues who might know something about the subject – for instance, if you are about to interview the new manager of Leeds United, talk to the sports editor or one of the football writers.

The importance of research cannot be emphasised enough. Fiammetta Rocco (in Glover 2000: 52), for instance, is meticulous about leaving no possible research stone unturned:

> If you are writing about someone who has a high public profile, much information is already publicly available. In addition to files of old cuttings and earlier interviews, company records, share deals, charity work, court documents and property records are just some of the many documents that are available to anyone who knows where to look. Far from being dusty piles of paper, these records, if you study them carefully, can tell you an awful lot about someone's personality.

Approaching an interviewee from a position of knowledge puts you, as a journalist, in a much stronger position than if you had done no research at all. However, it is important to recognise that the amount of research and preparation you need to do will vary according to the length and importance of the story, so, before you do anything else, you need to find out how much room there is on the page for the piece you are about to write – should it be an 800-word feature or a 200-word story? This will influence the number of questions you ask and the amount of time you spend on the interview.

SETTING UP

Having decided to do an interview, you need to fix a date and time that is convenient to both you and the interviewee. When setting a date, ask yourself: 'Am I giving myself and the interviewee enough time to prepare?' When setting a time, allow yourself enough time to travel there, get the information you need and then travel back to the office to write the story. If the interviewee is busy, he or she might only allow you a short time anyway – say, 20 minutes – and, in the case of a visiting celebrity, who is plugging their latest film, book or CD, you will be given a strict time limit because there will be a public relations officer (PRO) controlling proceedings and a line of journalists interviewing the same person before and after you. Interviews like this are what *The Observer*'s Lynn Barber (in Glover 2000: 204) describes as the

> ... absolute hell side of interviewing ... the hotel-room circus where a Hollywood star has flown into London for a day to talk non-stop about their latest film ... They are dazed with talking, hoarse with talking, often literally mad with talking – they gabble half the plot of the film and half the anecdote, they repeat whole paragraphs, they can never remember the question and they jump like startled deer if you ask a question they have never encountered before.

The upside of a barely coherent interviewee, however, is that it allows writers scope to be creative in order to, as Barber (in Glover 2000: 199) says, 'fill the gap between the three interesting sentences the star has uttered and the 3000-word article needed to provide a selling magazine cover story'. That, as Barber freely admits, can be terrific fun.

FACE-TO-FACE INTERVIEWS

Such interviews are best if you want to establish a rapport with the interviewees, which you will want to do if you are writing a feature or profile about them or if the subject is particularly sensitive. It also helps if they want to show you reports, documents or charts that would be unwieldy or impossible to fax or e-mail or if they need to draw a diagram to help explain a point.

Face-to-face interviews are more personal than other types of interviews as you can pick up on not just body language but also surroundings. How many features have you read that start off with a comment about how interviewees are dressed or a description of their homes, offices or restaurants in which the interviews are being held? A colleague's profile of Ian Byatt, former director general of the water regulator, OFWAT, began with a couple of paragraphs about some large and colourful paintings that adorned the walls of his office on the fifteenth floor of the Birmingham headquarters. She admired them on arrival (even though they were not really to her taste) and Byatt told her that he had painted them himself. Flattery not only broke the ice but also got her a colourful intro.

WHERE?

You need to find a convenient location for a face-to-face interview – convenient, that is, to both of you. Your interviewee needs to feel comfortable, relaxed and able to talk freely and openly, so you might want to do the interview in his or her office or at a location he or she suggests.

However, you need to make sure that wherever you meet is convenient for you, too. Can you get there easily and on time? Once there, will you be interrupted (a hazard if you meet in the interviewee's office)? If you meet in a pub or restaurant, will you be able to ask questions, take notes and drink and/or eat at the same time? A colleague who was writing a profile of actress Patricia Hodge agreed to interview the star at a restaurant in London, whereupon Ms Hodge was treated by the waiting staff with all due respect and, it has to be said, some servile deference, while the reporter (who was picking up the tab) was treated with unconcealed scorn. The interviewer found that the batteries had gone flat in her mini tape recorder, so she had to rely on shorthand notes made in an exercise book that was too big for the space between her Waldorf salad and the bread basket, and she had to field constant interruptions from the waiter.

Freelance magazine writer Carole Richardson also eschews lunchtime interviews: 'If I go out to lunch, I can't help asking questions – I can't just have lunch and interview them afterwards.' Instead, she prefers to interview her subjects in their own homes. This is because the magazine features she writes often have a very personal dimension – triumph over tragedy (TOT)-type features, of the sort that Australian communications lecturer John Langer (2000: 121) describes as victim stories that 'rely on devices to produce sympathetic responses through emotional engagement'. The aim is to draw on the interviewee's emotional responses to a personal tragedy in order to strike a sympathetic chord with readers. Although Langer refers specifically to the construction of television news victim stories, the analogy remains true for the female consumer magazine genre. For Richardson, this means that interviews can often be quite an emotional experience as interviewees relive a very personal tragedy and a safe, familiar environment helps to create the right sort of atmosphere: 'It helps people feel more comfortable and they open up to you more easily.'

On the other hand, if the interviewee is a powerful managing director or an important councillor or other dignitary, you, as an interviewer, do not want them to feel either too comfortable or too much in control. A neutral environment, the coffee lounge of a hotel or a quiet bar, might be more appropriate.

Regardless of location, however, having arranged a face-to-face interview:

- turn up suitably dressed
- be on time
- be polite and
- introduce yourself.

How you dress is important because, while it might be appropriate to be in jeans, sweatshirt and trainers for a feature on street crime, this is not the way to look when interviewing a lord mayor or the chairwoman of the WI. Getting a good interview often relies on gaining the interviewee's trust and, sorry to say, how you look will help, hinder or influence this process.

Being on time is important. Arriving late and offering breathless apologies for flat tyres and broken-down buses is not going to impress your interviewee. Apart from anything else, turn up late and they might have gone. Take a mobile phone with you and ring ahead if you are unavoidably late. (The mobile phone will also help if you are lost and in need of directions.)

Be polite at all times – even if the interviewee is rude or hostile. Press your questions firmly and be persistent, but never lose your cool or your temper.

Introducing yourself is vital as, unless you are doing an undercover investigation, the person you are interviewing must know who you are, which newspaper you work for or if you are freelance and what you are writing about.

You must take control of the interview. Media training of members of the public, especially people in positions of power and authority, instructs interviewees to take more control during an interview so that they are able to put across only those points that they want to put across. Be aware of this and take control yourself so that you ask the questions that elicit the answers you need for your story. In most interviews, though, it will be expected that the interviewer will take control. In fact, journalists are frequently asked, 'What do you need from me? What would you like me to do?'

INTERVIEWS ON THE PHONE

Cost-cutting and increased pressures on time in the newsroom mean that more and more interviews are done over the phone. The phone interview can be impersonal – there is no chance to pick up on body language, certain nuances of speech might be missed – when one of you is being funny, ironic or evasive, for instance – and there is a danger that one of you might be misheard or misunderstood.

However, the plus points are that busy people might be persuaded to do an interview if it is only going to involve a short phone call. Also, the telephone is a familiar medium and the interviewee, if interviewed on the phone in his or her office, will feel more relaxed than if meeting at a venue unknown to him or her.

You need to do just the same sort of preparation for this type of interview as one done face to face and ask the same types of questions. The advantage to you is that you can have a list of questions and background notes in front of you as prompts.

When you first ring, make sure that you are put through to the right person – it does happen that journalists waste time asking questions of the wrong Eric Jones.

Double-check spellings – on the phone a P sounds like a B and an F can be mistaken for an S, for instance.

There are certain things every journalist needs when interviewing people. A spiral bound notebook is best for ease and convenience. Always carry two ballpoint pens with you (in case one dries up) and a pencil. (If it rains – pencils work better than ink in the wet. Don't assume that interviews will always be conducted indoors – there are plenty of times when you will have to doorstep – that is, interview someone on the run – in the cold and the pouring rain.)

Tape recorders are small, easy to use and affordable, but batteries can run out, the thing might not record for some reason, external noise might drown out the interview and the tape you use might not last the length of the interview. There is also the problem of transcribing a lengthy interview from tape – do you have the time to listen to the whole tape to find one or two nuggets? Also, there are certain areas where tape recorders are not allowed, such as courts and council meetings, and certain interviewees who are wary of talking in front of tape recorders. If you do use a tape recorder, always make backup notes.

Shorthand is vital for accurate note-taking. The NCTJ and most other training bodies insist on 100 words per minute. Pitmans and Teeline are the two most popular systems. You will find that many journalists have attained their 100 wpm but take notes in a personal mix of short- and longhand that they develop over the years.

HOW LONG WILL THIS TAKE?

One of the commonest questions asked by an interviewee prior to giving an interview is 'How long will this take?' Once you have explained who you are and why you want to do the interview, it helps if you can give them notice of how long the process will last, as in 'I'll only take up 20 minutes of your time ...'

Again, the length of time needed for an interview will depend both on the type of story being written and the nature of the interviewee. An interview with a classroom assistant for a hard news story about a one-day strike by Unison trade union members will not require the same probing or sensitivity as a feature interview with a mother recalling the death of her child in a drink-driving accident.

Experience helps, too. When Carole Richardson first became a freelance journalist, a typical feature interview would take up to four hours:

I have a very set formula for interviewing. I go through the story chronologically from beginning to end, but I get them to give a lot more detail. For instance, how did they feel? What were they thinking? I also have an idea in the back of my mind of how I want the story to be – there's a clear beginning, middle and end. Some interviews can still take a long time, but, in general, I don't spend as long as I used to do.

It is a good idea to warn the interviewee in advance if you are taking a photographer along with you or if a photographer will contact him or her at a later date to arrange to take a picture.

THE QUESTION IS ...?

Having worked out who you are going to interview and the subject that you are going to interview them about, work out a list of questions and either keep them in your head or write them down. Journalists new to interviewing might find it helpful to have a list of questions in their note-books that they can tick off as each one is asked. If you are going to do this, write the questions on a separate page so that you can keep referring back to them easily and without causing too much distraction.

A list of questions will also be useful if you suddenly dry up and can't think of anything to say. Even the best journalists find that their minds go blank from time to time. However, having made a list, do not stick doggedly to it. You need to listen carefully to the answers and respond to them as appropriate.

Denis MacShane (1979: 124), a former journalist and trade unionist, now a Labour MP, describes interviewing as a circular conversation that covers the same ground many times in that journalists 'keep coming back to a subject, each time from a slightly different angle, in the hope that you will provide a give-away sentence which gives the reporter either the informa-tion she/he is looking for or a quote to make the story more exciting'.

In a sense, he is perfectly correct – journalists often do approach a sub-ject from more than one angle in order to gain new insights. However, it is a little disingenuous to liken the process, as MacShane (1979: 124) does, to a negotiation session. '... they [journalists] approach the goal by different routes in the hope that as one question (or negotiator's argument) fails another will unlock the answer (or the boss's coffers)'.

Posing a question in a different way often elicits a different response, but most journalists see themselves as what the late Robin Day described as humble seekers after truth and, rather than trying to score points, for most journalists the prize is a better, more rounded story that illuminates every facet of a, perhaps, quite complicated situation (Masterman 1994: 167).

Nevertheless, MacShane's circular conversation definition is an interesting one – not least because it implies a participatory experience to which both interviewee and interviewer contribute. Although all interviewers should remember that they have two ears and one mouth and should use them in similar proportions, the notion of a conversation suggests that one is listening in a supportive, non-threatening and genuinely interested way. This is important – not just because it encourages the interviewee, but also because it means that your questions will spring directly from what has just been said. Logical, relevant questions demonstrate that you are taking note of the interviewee's responses, not simply following a hidden agenda – which is the impression that can sometimes be given by a line of questioning that appears to have no relevance to the interviewee's previous sentence.

Also, of course, listening carefully means that an interview can often turn a story on its head. A journalist sets out on story A, but, during the interview, story B materialises because of the answers the interviewee is giving.

Bruce Smith, a senior reporter on the *Yorkshire Evening Post*, recalls a story that he was covering concerning the violent murder of an assistant coroner's wife:

> While interviewing a next-door neighbour, I naturally asked where the assistant coroner was to be found. She, apparently shocked at my ignorance, delighted in telling me that he had just been fished out of the canal. It later transpired that he had murdered his wife and committed suicide after partners in the solicitors' practice where he worked confronted him about irregularities in clients' financial affairs. It was suggested he had been spending clients' cash to fund his wife's expensive tastes.

So, while it is important to prepare for an interview with an idea, outline or list the questions you want to ask, be prepared to go off piste. Listen to the answers you are being given and pick up on them if they look as though they will lead somewhere more interesting than the route you had originally planned.

> During the interview, as you are noting the answers, score a line beside or highlight in some other way particularly interesting points as you write them down. This will help when you get back to the office and start writing the story. The intro and angle of the story should be bubbling in your mind as the interview is going on, but particularly useful quotes and points will be easier to find if you foreground them in some way as the interview progresses. With deadlines looming, you might not have time to transcribe every word of your notes, so knowing exactly where to look for a particular nugget will be helpful.

MORE QUESTIONS

Keep your questions clear and as concise as possible. Avoid multiple questions such as 'Where were you born? Did you go to school there and do you ever go back?' It is confusing and, while the interviewee might remember to answer two of them, the nugget might be in the third, unanswered, point. Avoid asking questions that result in a 'yes' or 'no' answer, such as 'Do you enjoy your work?' Interviewees should be encouraged to give full, rounded statements. You can best get these by asking open-ended questions. Start questions with who, what, when, why or how. For instance, 'What is it about your work that you enjoy/hate the most?' or 'Tell me about ...'.

Ask questions chronologically. That is not to say this is how you will write the story, but it offers another way of ticking off questions: early life – tick; first job – tick; present-day achievements – tick; now the future...?

If the interviewee is going off the subject, avoiding the questions, waffling or simply becoming boring, ask questions that pull him or her back on track.

Don't be in a rush to ask questions – be cool, calm and in control. Also, avoid interrupting – unless the interviewee is going off in a meaningless direction.

ENCOURAGING YOUR INTERVIEWEE

Use lots of signs, such as nodding and smiling, to encourage the interviewee to talk. As mentioned before, ask lots of questions and be interested.

The reluctant, nervous or genuinely shy interviewee is a tricky subject and needs to be handled with care. Reporter Sarah Carey, of the *Batley News*, tries to put such people at their ease by getting the formalities out of the way first:

> I ask them how their name is spelled, their address and age. If it is a birthday or anniversary I congratulate them or wish them well and then I mention something unrelated, such as the weather, just to start the conversation going. I do this because, for many people, especially when you are working on local papers, it will probably be the first time that they have been interviewed and it eases them in gently.

In fact, simply persuading such people to agree to an interview in the first place requires both skill and diplomacy. One solution can be to try and present the reason for your visit as offering the interviewee some sort of gain. This should not be done in a clumsy, clearly dishonest or insincere way. Bruce Smith says:

> Even in the most difficult, traumatic or sensitive situations, the publication of material supplied in an interview can offer help that may appeal to the interviewee. However, the advantage to the interviewee must not be overstressed as it will sound too much like a sales pitch.

In a tragic context, offering help may take the form of a simple suggestion to a recently bereaved person that reporting the death of a loved one could inform friends and acquaintances and reduce the distress that they may later suffer of being approached by people unaware of what has happened. Like many reporters, I have made gallons of tea for, and offered genuine sympathy to, people in such sad situations.

One tactic that some journalists use with a reluctant interviewee is to leave a gap between the last answer and their next question into which the interviewee sometimes slides. The interviewee works on the conversational convention that there should not be a silence and so they continue talking when things go quiet. It is at such times that they often let their guard down and say something that produces a nugget.

GENERAL DEMEANOUR

Avoid being arrogant, angry, facetious, sarcastic, diffident, shy or vague. Don't show off or argue with your interviewee either – an interview is not about you and your talents and opinions. You only need to display your own personality or intelligence if it will help win over an otherwise reluctant interviewee or if it will help relax and elicit more from him or her.

Be encouraging, sympathetic and polite. Empathy and respect are also important. Carole Richardson offers the following advice:

> I'm fascinated by human nature and, I suppose, naturally quite nosey, so I enjoy interviewing people and chatting to them. In some ways, as a mother of three, I often feel more of an empathy and closeness with the people I'm interviewing than I do with some other journalists.
> The important thing is to treat people with respect and not ridicule them – just treat them the way you would want to be treated yourself.

Equally importantly, you need to be interested. Bruce Smith says being genuinely interested – or at least appearing to be so – is the one principle he endeavours to apply to all interviews:

> I believe that this approach should be applied on every occasion to both encourage the interviewee and gain their trust. One should be interested in that person and their life, so as not to come over as someone only interested in talking to them to get information for a story. Unless an interviewer is careful, this can quickly happen. It may seem obvious, but sometimes one comes across reporters who fail to remove a glazed expression from their faces when trying to extract information.

Many journalists respond almost instinctively to the person they are interviewing by adapting their body language and vocabulary to make the interviewee feel more comfortable. This is not, as some might suggest, a cynical ploy to lure people into revealing more than they intended. Instead, for Sarah Carey it is an unconscious response:

> For example, if I am speaking to someone who has been having problems with their neighbours on a council estate and they speak quite broadly with a limited vocab, I try to cut out long words and speak in a similar manner to them. Similarly, if I am speaking to a councillor, I try to 'flex' my vocab and use my telephone voice. I don't do it intentionally, but if people see you as being on the same level as them, they tend to open up.

Often nuggets are to be found at the end of an interview. The journalist thanks the interviewee, closes the notebook, puts away the pen, shakes hands and heads for the door. The interviewee will then often relax at this point and say something that they had been trying to avoid during the formal part of the interview, such as: 'Oh, I thought you were going to ask me about ...'

They also save until the end of the interview the nugget that they had not realised was a good story. Very few interviewees have had journalism training and therefore do not realise that what is of little consequence to them is front-page news to us.

At the end of the interview double-check the spellings of names and places, check ages, marital status and titles.

Ask the interviewee if there is anything he or she wishes to add and leave your number in case they think of something. Check that you have their contact numbers and e-mail addresses in case you think of something else you want to ask or need to check anything with them. Says Sarah Carey: 'It can be a bit daunting phoning up after an interview and admitting that you have missed something, but most people don't mind. After all, they would prefer it to go into the paper correctly and are more likely to be upset if you get it wrong.'

QUESTIONS SENT IN ADVANCE

Some interviewees will ask if they can have a copy of your questions in advance. You do not have to do this, but if there is no other way of getting the person to talk, it might be something that you have to do. Few of our colleagues have ever been asked to do this, apart from when interviewing royalty or senior politicians. One who was asked, offered an outline of the interview subject areas rather than specific questions and this was accepted.

CAN I SEE IT BEFORE IT'S PRINTED?

In the same vein, you will find that many interviewees ask to see the finished copy before it goes into the paper. Do not show it to them. They will generally criticise it, change quotes and make alterations that invariably add grammatical errors. The time it takes for them to send it back also means that it could make you miss your deadline.

However, do recognise that, sometimes, compromises might have to be made. Fiammetta Rocco (in Glover 2000: 52), admits to sometimes checking quotes: '... if that's the deal ... [but] ... I never show anyone copy before publication. Ever. It leads to nothing but problems'.

If the interviewee is a specialist – for instance, a doctor or scientist – you might want to send him or her certain paragraphs of a highly medical or scientific nature to check for accuracy. Alternatively, you might consider giving an outline over the phone of what you have written. However, the only time an interviewee should automatically see the copy before it is printed is in the case of an advertorial for which they have paid. Otherwise, all editorial control lies with your editor.

THE E-MAIL INTERVIEW

Interviewing by e-mail is a growing phenomenon. It is quick and easy and some people respond better to e-mailed questions than they would to a face-to-face or telephone interview.

E-mail interviews work best where the information you need is factual rather than contentious; where you are expecting lots of detail but not planning to put your interviewee against the ropes.

A journalist relying on an e-mail interview needs to be aware that they might have to wait longer for the answers – and that could be a problem with tight deadlines. On the other hand, e-mail interviews give respondents time to think about their answers, so it could be argued that those answers will be better for the eventual story.

There is less chance of misquoting someone if you use their e-mail answers. It is easier to cut and paste their e-mailed remarks into your copy than transcribe your shorthand notes or tape recording.

Be aware that some e-mail answers purportedly from one person might have been composed by a committee or a PRO on his or her behalf – you have no way of knowing.

IN CONCLUSION, WHY DO IT?

Because, as mentioned earlier, interviews are the best way to get answers to the questions that, ultimately, will lead to the best story. Cynics such as Denis MacShane might imply that interviewers are coldly manipulative, interested only in securing a scoop, but personal experience suggests otherwise. Yes, we want the scoop (and, preferably, the front-page splash, too), but most of the journalists we know are more concerned with representing faithfully and truthfully the people who have allowed them into their lives. Most of us recognise how privileged we are to meet and be exposed to such a diversity of experience.

The last word on interviewing rests with Lynn Barber (in Glover 2000: 204–5):

> The joy of interviewing is almost infinite. I remember, particularly, a lunch with Rudolf Nureyev under a vine trellis in Lake Como – his strange accent, his enormous vocabulary and knowledge of books, his physical fragility (I didn't know it, but he was soon to die of Aids), his nostalgia for his early days in London, his pain in talking about his childhood in Ufa, his astonishing knowledge of plumbing and the problems of installing a desalination plant on his island off Naples (I remember thinking even at the time, 'My God, this is Nureyev, teaching me the difference between a reservoir and a cistern and a holding tank'), the extraordinary breadth of his enthusiasm and interest … I can think of dozens such interviews where, even while I worried about my next question and whether the tape would run out, I was aware that I was experiencing a golden privilege.

Exercise

1 You are a trainee reporter on the *Leodis Leader* – a weekly newspaper – and are about to set off on your first major interview. Write a list of things you need to check:

   a before you set off for the interview
   b what you need to do during the interview.

2 You are a reporter on the *Leodis Leader* – a weekly newspaper – and have received the following tip-off:

(Continued)

Exercise   (Continued)

Earlier today, shop assistants at the All-You-Want-For-A-Pound store on the High Street apprehended a teenage shoplifter. Police told them that they had no officers available to take the youth into custody and suggested the assistants parade him in front of the store's CCTV cameras and then release him. Police said that they would be able to identify and arrest him later.

Your news editor wants a 250-word story for this week's front page. Who do you want to interview and what questions would you ask?

(Answers are given at the end of the book.)

11

ONLINE JOURNALISM

The electronic age has changed our lives as communicating human beings. New methods of sending and receiving information enable us to communicate with a bank or supermarket, interrogate a library catalogue or encyclopedia database, or select from a series of menus, as in television data displays (Teletext). In each case, we have to learn new conventions of communications …

David Crystal, *The Cambridge Encyclopedia of the English Language* (1995: 392)

Increasingly journalists have to produce copy for online versions of their newspapers. This chapter looks at the ways in which writing for the Internet differs from writing for print and how language and content have to reflect the needs of a different reading environment.

In the early days of the Internet, regional journalists tended to have mixed views about online versions of their newspapers. While some regarded them as an asset, others saw them as technological gimmickry that might take readers, and thus circulation, away from their main paper product. In fact, after the initial big bang, most regional titles have cut back on their online output. Nevertheless, David Jackson, new media manager for the Yorkshire Weekly Newspaper Group (YWNG), is convinced that online newspapers have an important function, bolstering readership figures for his company's family of publications. He believes that readers use the two products in very different ways, dipping into the Web version to get updates on breaking stories and buying the printed paper at the end of the week for background information and detail:

> So, although most of the online stories have already appeared in the main newspaper, we do carry some new stories. For instance, when [multiple murderer] Harold Shipman hanged himself in Wakefield jail, our *Wakefield Express* website was the first, along with the BBC, to have that story. At the end of the week, the print paper carried a new piece adding additional information to move the story along.

The other benefit, of course, is that readers from further afield can keep abreast of local affairs without having to wait days for their paper to pop through the mailbox. 'We have guest boxes on all our sites,' says Jackson, 'and it is clear that our stories are being read throughout the UK as well as the rest of the world.' In fact, after a change of server put one of the company's newspapers offline for a week, the editor was inundated with e-mail and phone call complaints. It is proof, says Jackson, that online newspapers have become an integral part of the regional newspaper package: 'They've really caught on, I think, partly because they provide an element of interactivity and people like that. They like being able to look things up on the website and getting updates as things happen.'

JUST ONE MORE FIX

Jackson puts his finger firmly on two important truths here – interactivity and immediacy, both of which have significant implications for reader and journalist alike. In a 24-hour information society, where readers have come to expect instant access to national and international news, local news providers are under pressure to deliver the same level of service. The daily or weekly news fix offered by regional dailies, evenings and weeklies is no longer enough. 'Updates,' says Jackson, 'they're the key.'

In essence, good sites work with the paper product – and vice versa. Accordingly, at local election time, David Ward, editor of the *Pontefract and Castleford Express*, sends a reporter to cover the end-of-poll count:

> We could pick them up afterwards because the count takes place after we have gone to press, which means it would be too late for us to get the voting figures into that week's paper. Instead, we put the results on the website so that next morning people can find out who has got in and who has been voted out.
>
> Similarly, if we pick up a crime incident on Monday morning, an attack or a robbery, where police are appealing for information, we put it on the website. When the paper comes out later in the week, we carry an update, perhaps focusing on how responses from our readers have helped police with their investigations.
>
> It's part of our community service role to get things like that on the Internet straight away, but it also provides us with a more colourful story.

A LITTLE LIGHT RELIEF

This ability to respond quickly to breaking news is perhaps one of the greatest advantages that online journalism offers its readers – the elimination of the fixed news deadline. Because websites can be updated as and when news breaks, the information flow is dictated not by the production schedule of a particular news organisation, but by the speed at which a website provider can key in new details. You do not have to be a news junkie to recognise that such immediacy will change – indeed, has already begun to change – journalism in ways that we do not yet always fully appreciate. As the Internet becomes the primary provider of 'new' news, the traditional print media – the role of which as a first source has already been undermined by the broadcast media – must evolve still further as a vehicle for analysis, comment and detail.

It is a formula with which regional weeklies have long been familiar. Unable to compete with the dailies and evenings as a venue for new stories, they have always offered a more varied mix of detail and depth, with what David Ward describes as a leavening of humour and light relief. Personal columns and opinion pieces have become a staple and, while he sometimes worries that there is too much opinion in newspapers, readers cannot seem to get enough of it. The weekly lifestyle column he writes featuring his wife and cats has, he admits: 'Made Mrs W. a bit of a cult in Castleford.'

GUIDES NOT GATEKEEPERS

However, while traditional media are evolving to meet the competitive challenges presented by the Internet, journalism has not yet begun to fully exploit the opportunities provided by the new medium – in particular, its capacity for interactive engagement. For readers (consumers?), this represents one of its most appealing – and empowering – attributes. It is also, for journalists, a problematic one as even the most unsophisticated news sites contain an element of interactivity (simply clicking on one story rather than another involves a conscious action on the part of the reader). Journalists are no longer dealing with passive consumers swallowing a wholesome diet of facts and opinion. Instead, readers are actively involved in determining what items they read onscreen and the order in which they read them. Stuart Minting, who works on the news desk at Web-based news service Ananova, agrees: 'The people who use Ananova tend to read down through the headlines in the sections that they are most interested in.'

For the journalist, this means a fundamental change in role. Traditionally, the journalist has assumed the role of gatekeeper – opening and closing the news gateway to what he or she considers likely to be the most interesting and useful to readers. The impossibility of passing on everything journalists might know about a particular issue or event required them to make decisions about what readers did and did not need to know in order to function effectively in a modern world. However, as online journalist Steve Yelvington (Ward 2002: 26) observes, such a role becomes redundant in a world awash with information sources:

> You can't stop the flow of information. What you can do instead is to take the user or reader by the hand and lead them towards the light. I think we journalists have a function there, to sort through and point out. But more the function of a guide rather than a gatekeeper.

TO BLOG OR NOT TO BLOG

Up until now, we have talked about online news media solely as providers of traditional journalism. However, as journalists become guides rather than gatekeepers, the nature of the journalism provided – and the nature of the people doing the providing – is changing. Nowhere is this more evident than in the emergence of Web logs, or, blogs.

A relatively new phenomenon, they first began to emerge in significant numbers at the end of the twentieth century when the development of cheap software meant Web users could create personalised sites and update them regularly without the need for either technical or specialist expertise.

There is some evidence from the statements of early bloggers, and from the term 'Web log' itself, to suggest that such sites originally developed as a sort of personal online browsing record that the individuals concerned wanted to share with others. Gradually, these began to develop into what Donald Matheson, a lecturer at the School of Journalism, Media and Cultural Studies at Cardiff University, describes as online diaries, rich in hyperlinks to other sites. Most are written by a single person and, in true diary fashion, are chronologically organised. As such, unlike traditional journalistic offerings, they make no attempt to prioritise or rank information in order of importance. Nor are they necessarily particularly well written, and some are highly subjective, self-indulgent and opinionated.

INTERACTIVITY: A THREAT OR AN OPPORTUNITY?

Mike Ward, who led the development of an MA in online journalism at the University of Central Lancashire in Preston, sees blogging as an integral function of online interactivity. However, he says that interactivity is a process rather than a product and, like most processes, it can operate at different levels. The trick for the online journalist is to build the right level of interactivity into a site. Traditionally, as gatekeepers, journalists determined what was and was not newsworthy and presented the accompanying text to readers on a take-it-or-leave-it basis. As such, apart from the occasional letter or telephone call from readers, it was a predominantly one-way model.

Online journalism, however, offers more opportunity for readers to contribute – first, in terms of determining their own pathway through the material offered to them and, second, by making it easier for them to respond directly to individual journalists by means of e-mail addresses at the ends of bylined articles. As Mike Ward (2002: 145) says: 'Journalists are above all pragmatists. It only takes a couple of journalists to mention the great lead they have got on a story from a reader's e-mail to have the rest clamouring at the news editor's desk for the same opportunity.'

Additionally, Web logs offer another forum for canvassing ideas and opinions in terms of acting as what Steve Yelvington (Ward 2002: 46) describes as a test bed or sounding board where journalists can start a conversation with readers: 'Some may be well informed and some may be idiots, but the journalist can then participate in that conversation, and learn more, and out of that write a piece.'

However, the journalist at this point remains in the driving seat – any contributions from readers are filtered through them as professional mediators. Bloggers, however, together with newsgroups or message boards, make journalists redundant in the sense that users share information, offer insights and provide updates without the intervention of professional communicators. As we suggested earlier, although some of the material may be subjective and self-indulgent, some of it also provides an opportunity for journalists to tap into new and informed sources – sources, moreover, who may not only offer a fresh way of seeing but also deliver immediate, first-hand accounts of breaking news events. Additionally, such forums, says Mike Ward (2002: 148), are a useful way of tapping into users' needs, interests and preoccupations: 'Journalists are still engaged in the process but they have become users as well as providers.' In short, journalists are moving a step closer to their readers.

Clearly, the structure and format of Web logs varies according to the tastes and preferences of the individual creators. However, Web logger Rebecca Blood, author of Web logs *Rebecca's Pocket* and *The Weblog Handbook: Practical advice on creating and maintaining your blog* (2002), identifies two

(Continued)

(Continued)

broad categories of Web log: those that are short-form journals or diaries and those that emphasise their function as a conduit to what Mattheson describes as 'other paths of exploration'. Both, says Blood, perform useful functions. The conduit blogs, for instance, are a refinement of the original link-driven sites that, in their mix of 'links, commentary and personal thoughts and essays' (www.rebeccablood.net), encouraged readers to consider an alternative viewpoint or opinion. As such, they functioned not as didactic sources of information, but pointers, directing readers towards other material that might interest or engage them. Also, although such sites might include an irreverent and sarcastic commentary from the editors, they essentially act as what Blood calls 'filtering sites', pre-surfing the Web for readers. In that sense, they are guides rather than gatekeepers.

However, such sites are rapidly being superseded by the new short-form journal blogs that offer a record of the blogger's thoughts, opinions and observations about the world around them. 'These fragments,' says Blood, 'pieced together over months, can provide an unexpectedly intimate view of what it is to be a particular individual in a particular place at a particular time.'

CARRY ON SHOVELLING

Nevertheless, although such a willingness to engage directly with readers is becoming more common, in general, the potential for renegotiating traditional practices is, says Donald Matheson, hampered by the 'general conservatism and rigidity' of those practices. Although it is becoming increasingly common for journalists to attach personal e-mail addresses to features and opinion pieces, it remains relatively rare to attach such addresses to news stories. This conservatism extends to the structure and content of online versions of traditional publications. Most are little more than what some commentators disdainfully describe as shovel-ware – online versions of the print edition. While, structurally, there are good reasons for this, as we shall consider later in this chapter, contentwise, the failure to harness the technical potential of the Internet in terms of audio and visual aids might be considered perverse stagnation. Such a viewpoint, however, ignores the context of modern print journalism and the changes that have taken place within the industry in the last quarter of a century. We, and many of the people quoted in these pages, became reporters in the days of hot metal, we have weathered the introduction of photocomposition and have come to terms with direct inputting and onscreen subbing and layout. Journalists who have weathered such challenges are more than capable of also weathering the challenge of online newspapers, even if it remains unclear what part they play in the overall journalism package.

SYMBIOSIS

Interestingly, David Ward finds that a symbiotic relationship is developing between the two media. For instance, he regularly invites readers to take part in online polls: 'We had one recently on the urban renaissance of the two towns. We asked readers what they thought about it and the results of the vote provided a story in the paper about how many people were in favour of it.'

The paper also runs what Ward describes as a 'Can you help?' page:

> We might print an old picture and ask readers for help identifying it or, perhaps, someone who served in the Army 50 years ago asks for help to trace somebody from Castleford who served alongside him. Does anybody know the where-abouts of Bob Smith? The page only runs in the paper every four weeks, but it stays on the website for a full month. We usually get lots of responses and, again, that produces stories for the paper. It's the way of the future.

Ward's colleague Chris Page, editor of the *Selby Times*, has taken technology a step further. In a bid to involve younger readers, he encourages them to text him with news and views and runs text polls to gauge their reactions to community issues:

> I look at my daughter and her young friends and it's the way young people communicate with each other. If they've got something to say, they send a text and if we want to engage with younger readers we've got to use the media they use. We're getting a good response to it and I'm sure it will become much more widespread among other papers in the group.

NO MILEAGE IN AUDIO AND VISUAL AIDS – FOR NOW ...

For the moment, David Ward, for instance, sees it as his primary role to sell newspapers and the Internet edition of his newspaper represents a valuable tool with which to add readership and circulation and maximise revenues for the print publication. As such, the steps he has already taken towards encouraging interactivity are serving their purposes well. For now, though, there is no mileage to be gained from investing heavily in audio and visual aids. Accordingly, such 'gimmickry' remains largely the province of standalone Internet news sites, the revenue for which derives exclusively from the number of hits they receive. However, as with anything else, once readers become familiar with these interactive elements, they will begin to demand them from other providers. Ward and his colleagues will inevitably follow suit.

USERS OR READERS?

We keep referring here to the users of online journalism as readers, but, just as the relationship between reader and reporter changes online, so the relationship that readers enjoy with onscreen text is different. Although print encourages readers to be passive – to take what is placed in front of them and consume it according to a pattern dictated by the writer – most readers will also have some degree of engagement with the work in hand. A book, for instance, becomes un-put-down-able and newspaper readers look for the work of particular columnists or sports writers. Similarly, when David Jackson's online customers complained about not being able to access one of the YWNG news sites, their particular grumble was that they were unable to read that week's lifestyle column written by the paper's editor. A quirky, humorous look at life, the column is one of the publications must-read items: 'And people who usually access it online weren't very happy when they couldn't read it.'

In general, however, while readers are just as likely to pick up a newspaper and read it as much for pleasure as for information, their relationship with computers is more functional. While that may change (who knows where new technology and interactive television will take us in the future?) generally, reading online is a different experience to reading a newspaper. Scrolling down a computer screen to read a piece of text lacks the visceral pleasure associated with turning the pages of a broadsheet or a tabloid. It is also a lot more cumbersome – you cannot take a PC to the beach or read it in the bath.

Further, while the print resolution of a typical regional newspaper is never going to be as good as either a book or glossy magazine, it is still much better than that of a computer, where readers are typically sitting an arm's length from their screens. Colleagues who can read a newspaper without their varifocals struggle with an online text. In fact, people 'generally do not want to read long linear sections of material for enjoyment. Many readers even print out the material once they have located it electronically' (Bonime and Pohlmann 1998: 75).

In short, we are wedded to print – not least because reading from computer screens is approximately 25 per cent slower than reading from paper.

PEOPLE DON'T READ, THEY SCAN

All of this means, unfortunately, that a significant number of readers scan Web pages rather than read them in detail. This is a problem. As usability expert Steve King (Ward 2002: 128) observes: 'We're thinking "great literature" … while the user's reality is much closer to a billboard going by at 60 miles an hour.' Users want facts and they want them fast. They do not want erudite, wordy prose.

Stuart Minting, of Ananova, agrees: 'We tell new reporters to write short sentences where possible, avoid dropped intros at all costs – get straight to the point. Avoid tabloid slang, and, on the other end of the scale, lengthy words.' Otherwise, he says, usual newspaper rules apply: keep it short and simple:

> Writing for Ananova is probably most similar to writing for news agencies, where information should be presented in as succinct and clear a fashion as possible so people can disseminate the information with minimum effort. It's a tough discipline, but the key thing to remember is to be clinical – if it's not directly relevant, leave it out.

DOES SCANNING AFFECT NEWS VALUES?

Does this need to cater for the reader who scans rather than reads affect news values? For instance, are there stories that will be dropped because they will take too much explaining and others that will gain precedence because they can be written so that they are shorter and snappier? No, says Stuart Minting:

> All stories can be condensed to a single sentence or less if you choose – just like NIBs in newspapers. For example, we send news flashes to tens of thousands of people. One example would be, 'Plane crashes into World Trade Centre in New York. Terrorism suspected'. However important the story, it can be condensed. We keep all news stories to a 10-paragraph maximum. That is, almost always – except, perhaps an outstanding court case – ample to explain the tale.

YOU CAN'T BUY ATTENTION

Actually, newspaper readers do not want erudite, wordy prose either. David Gauntlett (Ward 2002: 3) points out: 'You can't buy attention … you can't make [people] interested in what you have to say unless they actually find the content of what you have to say engaging.'

In this respect, online journalism is no different from print journalism. Certainly, the fact that the stories posted on the YWNG news sites are identical to those that appear in the company's newspapers suggests that, structurally, what works for one works for the other. Well, yes and no.

LET ME TELL YOU A STORY …

First, at a very basic level, all journalism is about telling stories and, like all storytellers, a journalist needs to adapt style, tone, structure and content to meet the needs and expectations of his or her audience. It is one of the core principles of journalism. Accordingly, direct, accessible language is a prerequisite for both Web and print journalism – it is essential to grab the reader's attention and keep it by using strong headlines and clear, concise language that illuminates both purpose and content. Online journalist Leah Gentry (Ward 2002: 122–3) advocates: 'Careful and unbiased reporting, using compelling writing.'

The inverted triangle structure, using the intro as a hook to lure the reader in and gradually allowing the facts to unfold in order of importance, is ideally suited to the onscreen format. However, where a print journalist has only one tool – the written text – with which to communicate with readers, an online journalist, as we discussed earlier, can employ a multifaceted approach, using both audio and visual aids to allow 'both journalist and reader to do what they did before (e.g. access information) only more extensively and quickly' (Ward 2002: 18). Thus, the best online journalism combines the detail and background colour of the print media with the immediacy and vividness of the broadcast media.

NEW WAYS OF SEEING REQUIRE NEW WAYS OF WRITING

Andrew Bonime and Ken Pohlman (1998: 45–6) describe writing for new media as being akin to expressing ideas in the sort of random way that they are formed in our minds: 'Human thought consists of a linked network of individual ideas, recollections and images, many of which may be seemingly unrelated in content but have some relationship to the others.' While conventional print journalism delivers the news in a series of sequential links, the online journalist deconstructs the traditional storytelling process and reconstructs it into a series of independent but related storyboards.

HYPERTEXT

These storyboards are linked to each other by means of hypertext – words that are linked to other words that exist either in another part of the original document or another work altogether. Their purpose is to allow the online journalist to present ideas in a manner that more closely resembles the way we think. It 'allows ideas to be linked into a larger, more contextual whole' and allows writers 'to express ideas without having to adhere to the often constricting need to place them in a specific order' (Bonime and Pohlman 1998: 45–6). Significantly, in presenting ideas non-sequentially, hypertext allows readers to access a text in a way that suits their own particular needs and interests. How and what they consume becomes driven by the user rather than the provider. Bonime and Pohlman describe this process as being a bit like connecting ideas in the form of a web rather than a chain. The web of information spirals out from the centre in ever-increasing circles rather than heading rigidly in a pre-determined direction.

THE JOURNALIST AS NAVIGATOR

Accordingly, while a print journalist can exercise a measure of control over how and in what order pages are read – most readers will begin at page one and follow the story through sequential pages – the online journalist has no such luxury. The reader constructs as they go along, clicking on hypertext links (or ignoring them) as they choose fit. The writer, therefore, must act as a navigator, helping the reader to steer his or her way through the content in a logical and sensible way. While the print reader finds him- or herself presented with a single story, structured like an inverted triangle, and must plough through what doesn't interest him or her to find the stuff that does, the online reader is presented with a series of related but standalone stories, each linked by hypertext, that together constitute total coverage of an event or issue.

CHUNKING

This segmentation process is called chunking – it allows readers to scan a piece, identify what interests them and what does not and move on to the next chunk of information by clicking on the hypertext links. In this way, the online journalism provider can offer a much greater range and scope of material than a print journalist, for whom content is always determined by the fact that only a finite number of pages is available. On the other hand, the reader of a print piece knows from the beginning how much information is available – they can see how much there is to read. The online reader, though, has only a fragmented picture of what is available. It is much harder to get a sense of the whole.

I'VE READ THIS BEFORE

This has a number of consequences for the writer – he or she cannot be sure, for instance, that individual users will navigate through *all* the available chunks relating to a particular topic. Therefore, each chunk has to establish its place within the overall whole by summarising important elements of the central story without alienating the user who *has* read it all – the worst thing that can happen is for a reader to think: 'I've read this before.'

GUIDELINES FOR ONLINE JOURNALISTS

- Break the story into short, self-contained chunks. Each should deal with just one aspect of the bigger picture, so a report on the Iraq war might include a hard news chunk on a US helicopter crash, a colour piece from Saddam Hussein's home town of Tikrit, an in-depth analysis of the war so far, together with an opinion piece on the merits, or otherwise, of the campaign.
- Use the inverted triangle structure. Each chunk should start with the most interesting, dramatic or latest news. Expand and develop the points outlined in the intro, weaving background information into the fabric of the chunk before tying up any loose ends.
- Keep the language simple and direct. Use active rather than passive sentences and avoid short forms, such as can't, don't, won't. Instead, write cannot, do not, will not.
- Aim for no more than 30 to 40 words per sentence and a maximum of three sentences per par. Try to have a mix of longer and shorter sentences and pars – it creates white space onscreen and is easier on the eye.
- Insert a double linespace between pars and, unless a story is exceptionally important, each chunk should equate to no more than a page-and-a-half of A4 – around 500 or so words. Remember, onscreen, less is more.
- Use subheadings or crossheads and bulleted lists to break up the text.
- Use a standfirst (text under a headline offering extra information, often including a reporter's byline) to emphasise what is new or different about each chunk.
- Headlines and page titles should be simple, direct and informative. Avoid puns and ambiguities.
- Adapt the tone and voice to suit the subject matter – a story about six soldiers killed in a helicopter crash requires a different treatment from one about a reunion party for a group of Second World War veterans.
- Be positive rather than negative: the glass should be half full rather than half empty.
- Use concrete words and figures – a six-car pile-up rather than a multivehicle collision.
- Be careful about punctuation: commas, semi-colons and colons are all difficult to identify on screen. Use a dash instead – they stand out much better, which is especially important for someone reading from a small laptop screen. Full stops are less problematic because they are always (or ought to be) followed by a capital letter.
- Proofread carefully. Spot the difference between 'They survived in hospitable conditions' and 'They survived inhospitable conditions'.

HAVEN'T I HEARD THIS BEFORE?

The short answer is yes. The rules of good Internet writing are exactly the same as those applied to all good journalism. Content, style, tone and voice are all determined by the purpose of the piece – education, information, persuasion or entertainment – and by the needs and expectations of the reader. Whether writing for the Web or print, all journalists should bear in mind the advice that online journalist Steve Yelvington gives on his website (www.yelvington.com): 'Timely, useful, interactive, entertaining. Hit those notes and you succeed. Miss those notes and you fail.'

Exercise

Take the council planning story featured in Chapter 6 and rewrite it for the Web. Strip out unnecessary details – instead, these should be presented as a side-bar or as a link to another Web article. What further links might be included?

(Answers are given at the end of the book.)

THE JOURNALIST IN SOCIETY

I am not a correspondent, I am just a reporter. I offer no point of view.
I take no action. I don't get involved. I just report what I see.

Michael Caine, playing Thomas Fowler in
The Quiet American (2001)

This chapter

- considers the role of the journalist
- looks at journalistic ethics
- examines the constraints under which a journalist works
- studies how journalists are perceived and how they perceive themselves.

As Michael Caine's character, Thomas Fowler, says in the film, *The Quiet American* – based on the book of the same name by Graham Greene – his role is not that of a correspondent, with opinions of his own and plenty of comment to make; he is just a reporter who reports what he sees. So it should be. Reporters are not asked to do anything else. Newspaper readers do not necessarily want to hear about the private lives of reporters or read their opinions, they simply want the story.

In telling that story, however, a journalist does have an important role to play, whether the Michael Caine character likes it or not, and that role carries responsibilities, some of which the journalist will acknowledge consciously, some unconsciously, and some not at all.

WHAT IS THE JOURNALIST'S ROLE?

Many journalists would say that their role is to listen and observe. Others would add that they should also inform, educate and, even, entertain. Some would suggest that we do too much of the latter. David Todd, assistant editor of the *Sheffield Star*, dislikes the modern trend towards celebrity gossip and trivia:

> A lot of local papers have gone too far down that road and left behind what we ought to be doing, which is to get the facts in the right order and leave it to the reader to make decisions about how important the story is. The place for exciting colourful material is in a feature and a news story should be written straight.

Some trainee journalists believe that the media is a glamorous place to be, that journalism is a career in which they can shine and find praise and recognition, but the reality is that reporters are more likely to be criticised for their work than patted on the back. Only a few reporters in the vast world of journalism find fame and are known and recognised for their work. The majority of journalists simply get on with the job and get on with it fairly anonymously. Reporting is foot-slogging hard work with little pay, yet, despite this, good reporters keep turning up enthusiastic, self-motivated and determined. They find their satisfaction in hearing, seeing and reporting on events that few people have seen and in situations where the public often has no access, and they pass on that information in the most honest and appropriate way. They find great satisfaction in seeing their byline in print, but it could be argued that bylines are for journalists only; that the readership takes little notice of them. So, if you want to be a celebrity, find something else to do.

ESSEX, EFFICKS, EFFEX - WOT'S THIS ETHICS THEN?

Kelvin Mackenzie, one of Fleet Street's most infamous editors, once remarked (Hargreaves 2003: 211): 'Ethics is a place to the east of London where the men wear white socks.' The inference is clear: ethics has no place in journalism – or, at least, in the journalism practised by those cast in the Mackenzie mould. Hand on heart, neither of us can say that we have never come across his ilk, but, thankfully, they are the exception rather than the rule – especially in the provinces where even those journalists with Fleet Street (or should that be Canary Wharf?) ambitions are rooted in the communities in which they serve. Note that word 'serve' because many trainees, when asked why they want to be journalists, say that they 'want to make a difference', 'they want to right wrongs' or 'they want to expose scandals'.

However, while it is no bad thing to have ideals, a dose of realism is required, too. In your first job on a local or regional newspaper, you might feel that there is fraud and double dealing going on in every corner, but, in actual fact, you are more likely to be engaged in writing up reports about local events and characters that pose no great threat to world peace. Of course, you must be alert for wrongdoing, bad practice and downright lying while on a story and expose it where necessary and appropriate, but the chances are that most of the stories you will be working on will involve local people doing (hopefully) honest and (generally) worthwhile things in the community rather than plotting to bring down Queen and country. In that context, working ethically – and being seen to be working ethically – will help a newspaper to build up trust with its readers, which is something that Debbie Hall, assistant publications editor for Hull Daily Mail Publications, says is the key to operating successfully within a community:

As a journalist, I believe that I carry a responsibility both to my readers and to the people I interview. I start by being polite and respectful and treating them how I would like them to treat me. I've got more stories by doing that than I would have done by being brusque or rude.

For instance, one of the first stories I covered when I came to Hull 18 years ago was an interview with a chap who has subsequently become the city's longest-surviving heart transplant patient. I happened to meet him before the operation when he was very ill and couldn't even make it up the stairs of his house. There was lots to tell, but, because I didn't over-dramatise his story and told it in a sensitive way, he and his family have treated me like a pal ever since. They rang me from Papworth Hospital after the operation and took some pix and gave them to me and over the years they've been in touch every few months or so.

Some people think getting a story is all about an easy in and out, but this is a case in point. Eighteen years down the line, these people still relate to me and if anything ever happens, such as a health scare, and he's had a few of those, I get it.

You can't just walk in and walk out again. You've got to remember that you and what you write will have an impact on people.

THE SOHAM DILEMMA

This was certainly a consideration for staff at *The Ely Standard* when Soham schoolgirls Holly Wells and Jessica Chapman disappeared in

August 2002. The national and international media descended and swarmed in and around the town for nearly a fortnight as the search for the girls went on.

Soon after their bodies were found, school caretaker Ian Huntley was arrested and charged with the murder of the two girls, and his former girl-friend, Maxine Carr, was arrested and charged with conspiring to pervert the course of justice. Both were eventually convicted and sentenced, but, during the trial itself, the local paper, being highly sensitive to the fact that all the nationals were featuring the trial on their front pages, considered local opinion and restricted its coverage to the inside pages. In an editorial, the paper explained why:

> *The Standard*, in an attempt to reflect the wishes of the community and be less intrusive, has decided not to run any court copy on its front pages until there is a verdict in the case.
>
> We will be following the trial, but reporting will be published on inside pages only. Our billboards will also not contain any references to the trial.

Deputy editor Debbie Davies says it had been a hard decision that went against all her journalistic principles:

> It was one of the biggest stories ever for us and the natural instinct was to put it on the front page, but I created a scenario in my head where I could see the parents of the two little girls coming home from the court day after day and they did not want to see our billboards screaming at them or go into the local shop and see front page headlines in *The Standard*.

Instead, the local paper devoted its front page to stories that it would otherwise normally carry, with a box referring to the trial on inside pages:

> Some other journalists were quite sneering. They said we were being naïve and parochial, but we were very aware of how the local community was feeling and my gut instinct was that we should be less intrusive. We still carried the trial inside the paper and we didn't duck any of the issues. We were not trying to sanitise the story in any way; we were simply doing something more aesthetic and less intrusive.

The paper, which carried messages of goodwill from readers while the girls were still missing, was flooded with tributes when their bodies were found. Davies says:

> We provided an outlet for the local community and something they could focus on. The whole situation gave us a chance to step back and ask, are we really in touch with the local community and giving them what they want? Maybe we should think more about how we report things instead of always treading the same well-worn path.

WHAT'S REALLY IN THE PUBLIC INTEREST?

Jon Grubb, editor of the *Scunthorpe Telegraph*, agrees. His view is that local and regional newspapers can be as insensitive as the nationals – particularly when covering inquests and death knocks:

> You find a lot of local and regional editors being quite critical of the nationals, but when a big story happens in your patch and the nationals get involved, there is a level of expectation that the story is going to get published. But with things like inquests and death knocks, particularly around children and babies, you have to ask yourself how intrusive are you being and is it in the public interest?
>
> We cover all the inquests but make a decision about which ones to publish once we know the facts. In general terms, if a man kills himself in the privacy of his own home because he was depressed that his wife had left him, my feeling would be that reporting it would not be in the public interest – no one has committed a crime and no one is to blame – but if a schoolboy was found hanged and there were possible issues relating to the pressure of exams or bullying, then there is public interest and a good reason to publish.
>
> My advice to local and regional editors is to put yourself in the shoes of the victim's family. If you can justify why it is a story, then publish, but if you can't, don't.
>
> I think that when a local or regional newspaper behaves insensitively, the local community feels that it has been betrayed by one of its own; local people feel let down.

A QUESTION OF MORALITY?

How sensitive can you afford to be, particularly with court cases where there is a public interest in reporting charges against a local character – albeit one who would rather not be spotlighted? It is an ethical dilemma faced every day by newspapers that report the courts, but one that had ramifications for the *Isle of Wight County Press*.

A local headteacher, Alastair Wilbee, killed himself in August 2003 after being named as a child abuse defendant. He had gone missing the day before a report of his first court appearance was due to appear in the *County Press*. A *Press Gazette* report quoted David Hart, of the National Association of Headteachers, as saying there was 'no doubt at all that Mr Wilbee's death was caused by the publicity he received'.

However, *County Press*'s editor, Brian Dennis, says that he treated Mr Wilbee as he would anyone else who was charged or appeared in court:

> I didn't think twice about naming him. He appeared in open court and was charged. We carried two or three pars of straightforward, factual reporting; we didn't dress it up in any way. No representation was made to me to keep his name out of the paper, but I wouldn't have done anyway. Part of our job is to report what goes on and there is a public interest in reporting that a headmaster has

appeared on charges like that. The moment you start making moral judgements about which cases to include and which to leave out, you are on a slippery slope.

If a headmaster came up tomorrow in similar circumstances, we would do the same again – if I didn't I'd be giving in to blackmail. By covering the case, we are not doing anything differently to any other newspaper – and if we hadn't covered it, people would have asked why not, what is going on?

As a local newspaper read by 94 per cent of the island, we are here as a mirror for the community. We have to record and reflect what the community is doing and what it is saying – and a mirror can't do anything but reflect things as they are.

In a sense, he is echoing the view of many regional journalists who firmly believe in the notion of journalism as a public service.

QUOTES

Trainee journalists often ask if they are allowed to change quotes. Well, the answer is obviously 'no, but …'. During the course of an interview, someone might give a reporter lots of information – some useful and usable, some sheer waffle and pointless. Whatever it is, the reporter is not going to be able to use it all, even if he or she did get it all down verbatim in a shorthand note. Nor would a newspaper be prepared to waste space with quotes that add nothing to the story. Some editing is required. Select appropriately the parts of the quote that you plan to use as direct speech, paraphrase other parts as reported speech and jettison the rest. Whatever you do, do not misrepresent or corrupt the meaning of what an interviewee has told you.

Some journalists are tempted to 'tidy up' grammatical errors in quotes – a process that they feel is kinder than using a (sic) to show the printed error is not theirs. General advice is to avoid this and perhaps put the quote in reported speech instead.

An old journalistic trick is to put words into the mouth of an uncommunicative or unhelpful interviewee, as in, 'Do you think this is an outrageous waste of taxpayers' money?' A 'yes' or 'no' reply is then quoted as direct speech, as in, 'I think this is an outrageous waste of taxpayers' money …'. Avoid doing this; try using reported speech instead.

Avoid giving unattributable quotes – for instance, 'A bus passenger said …' – always name your source if at all possible. Never make up quotes.

CAN I SEE IT BEFORE IT'S PUBLISHED?

Interviewees sometimes ask to see the copy before it is published and the general answer should be 'No'. There is a tendency among interviewees to edit copy sent for approval, take out parts that they do not like, change things that they regret saying and add information that could change the whole tone of the story. A reporter must be trusted to do his or her job, which means writing a fair, accurate and balanced story. Apart from anything else, copyright lies with the newspaper and no one outside the newspaper should see copy before it is published.

There may be occasions, however – particularly when writing highly complicated and difficult stories of, say, a technical or medical nature – when a reporter might want to send a particular passage to a specialist interviewee to check for correct spellings, terminology and errors.

PERKS, FREEBIES, FAVOURS AND INDUCEMENTS

Is there any such thing as a free lunch? Journalists are often sent perks and freebies – from a free ticket to a local pop concert to a two-week cruise on the Mediterranean. Perks and freebies are usually sent by a PRO or organisation hoping to win favourable coverage in your newspaper. To avoid being compromised, a reporter should always make it clear that any resulting copy from the concert or cruise will be written to normal journalistic standards, not be free advertising.

Reporters should avoid soliciting perks or freebies with promises of coverage in their newspaper because there are no guarantees that everything a reporter writes will go in the newspaper.

Favours can work positively for reporters, but they should choose the type of favour and the person with whom it is exchanged with care. Reporters look on favours done for a police officer, for instance, as an investment as they will be known when a future crime story materialises.

INVENTION

Do not invent anything.

PLAGIARISM

Do not plagiarise anyone else's material. Credit your sources and attribute your quotes.

CODE OF PRACTICE

It is all very well brandishing the sword of truth while walking the high moral ground as you go about your reporting duties, but it is worth turning your ethical principles inwards as well. Look at yourself as a journalist and journalism in general because, in much of the industry, when talking of ethics the reply is all too often: 'I haven't got time to think about that – I've got a paper to get out.'

The macho school of journalism, where it is reckoned that journalists can flout the law or publish and be damned, is still with us and, up to a point, it should be in the sense that certain rules and regulations should be tested and exposed as the nonsensical, unworkable things that they are. However, the press has a duty to maintain the highest professional and ethical standards and, while it is self-regulated, there is a code that sets the benchmark for those standards. The Code of Practice, produced by a committee of editors and ratified by the Press Complaints Commission, aims to protect the rights of the individual while upholding the public's right to know.

Last updated in May 2004, the Code has 16 sections and, because few journalists could have more than a vague stab as to what its contents are, it is worth printing them in full here.

THE EDITOR'S CODE OF PRACTICE

1 Accuracy
   i   The Press must take care not to publish inaccurate, misleading or distorted information, including pictures.

   ii   A significant inaccuracy, misleading statement or distortion once recognised must be corrected, promptly and with due prominence, and – where appropriate – an apology published.

   iii   The Press, whilst free to be partisan, must distinguish clearly between comment, conjecture and fact.

   iv   A publication must report fairly and accurately the outcome of an action for defamation to which it has been party, unless an agreed settlement states otherwise, or an agreed statement is published.

2 Opportunity to reply
A fair opportunity for reply to inaccuracies must be given when reasonably called for.

3 Privacy*
   i   Everyone is entitled to respect for his or her private and family life, home, health and correspondence, including digital communications. Editors will be expected to justify intrusions into any individual's private life without consent.

ii It is unacceptable to photograph individuals in private places without their consent.

Note – private places are public or private property where there is a reasonable expectation of privacy.

4 Harassment

i Journalists must not engage in intimidation, harassment or persistent pursuit.

ii They must not persist in questioning, telephoning, pursuing or photographing individuals once asked to desist; nor remain on their property when asked to leave and must not follow them.

iii Editors must ensure these principles are observed by those working for them and take care not to use non-compliant material from other sources.

5 Intrusion into grief or shock

In cases involving personal grief or shock, enquiries and approaches must be made with sympathy and discretion and publication handled sensitively. This should not restrict the right to report legal proceedings, such as inquests.

6 Children*

i Young people should be free to complete their time at school without unnecessary intrusion.

ii A child under 16 must not be interviewed or photographed on issues involving their own or another child's welfare unless a custodial parent or similarly responsible adult consents.

iii Pupils must not be approached or photographed at school without the permission of the school authorities.

iv Minors must not be paid for material involving children's welfare, nor parents or guardians for material about their children or wards, unless it is clearly in the child's interest.

v Editors must not use the fame, notoriety or position of a parent or guardian as sole justification for publishing details of a child's private life.

7 Children in sex cases

i The Press must not, even if legally free to do so, identify children under 16 who are victims or witnesses in cases involving sexual offences.

ii In any press report of a case involving a sexual offence against a child:

a the child must not be identified
b the adult may be identified
c the word 'incest' must not be used where a child victim might be identified
d care must be taken that nothing in the report implies the relationship between the accused and the child.

8 Hospitals*

i Journalists must identify themselves and obtain permission from a responsible executive before entering non-public areas of hospitals or similar institutions to pursue enquiries.

ii The restrictions on intruding into privacy are particularly relevant to enquiries about individuals in hospitals or similar institutions.

9 Reporting of crime
i Relatives of friends of persons convicted or accused of crime should not generally be identified without their consent, unless they are genuinely relevant to the story.
ii Particular regard should be paid to the potentially vulnerable position of children who witness, or are victims of, crime. This should not restrict the right to report legal proceedings.

10 Clandestine devices and subterfuge*
i The Press must not seek to obtain or publish material acquired by using hidden cameras or clandestine listening devices; or by intercepting private or mobile telephone calls, messages or e-mails; or by the un-authorised removal of documents or photographs.
ii Engaging in misrepresentation or subterfuge can generally be justified only in the public interest and then only when the material cannot be obtained by other means.

11 Victims of sexual assault
The Press must not identify victims of sexual assault or publish material likely to contribute to such identification unless there is adequate justification and they are legally free to do so.

12 Discrimination
i The Press must avoid prejudicial or pejorative reference to an individual's race, colour, religion, sex, sexual orientation or to any physical or mental illness or disability.
ii Details of an individual's race, colour, religion, sexual orientation, physical or mental illness or disability must be avoided unless genuinely relevant to the story.

13 Financial journalism
i Even where the law does not prohibit it, journalists must not use for their own profit financial information they receive in advance of its general publication, nor should they pass such information to others.
ii They must not write about shares or securities in whose performance they know that they or their close families have a significant financial interest without disclosing the interest to the editor or financial editor.
iii They must not buy or sell, either directly or through nominees or agents, shares or securities about which they have written recently or about which they intend to write in the near future.

14 Confidential sources
Journalists have a moral obligation to protect confidential sources of information.

15 Witness payments in criminal trials

i No payment or offer of payment to a witness – or any person who may reasonably be expected to be called as a witness – should be made in any case once proceedings are active as defined by the Contempt of Court Act 1981.

This prohibition lasts until the suspect has been freed unconditionally by police without charge or bail or the proceedings are otherwise discontinued; or has entered a guilty plea to the court; or, in the event of a not guilty plea, the court has announced its verdict.

ii Where proceedings are not yet active but are likely and foreseeable, editors must not make or offer payment to any person who may reasonably be expected to be called as a witness, unless the information concerned ought demonstrably to be published in the public interest and there is an overriding need to make or promise payment for this to be done; and all reasonable steps have been taken to ensure no financial dealings influence the evidence those witnesses give. In no circumstances should such payment be conditional on the outcome of the trial.

iii *Any payment or offer of payment made to a person later cited to give evidence in proceedings must be disclosed to the prosecution and defence. The witness must be advised of this requirement.

16 Payment to criminals

i Payment or offers of payment for stories, pictures or information, which seek to exploit a particular crime or to glorify or glamorise crime in general, must not be made directly or via agents to convicted or confessed criminals or to their associates – who may include family, friends and colleagues.

ii Editors invoking the public interest to justify payment or offers would need to demonstrate that there was good reason to believe the public interest would be served. If, despite payment, no public interest emerged, then the material should not be published.

* The public interest

There may be exceptions to the clauses marked * where they can be demonstrated to be in the public interest.

1 The public interest includes, but is not confined to:

    i detecting or exposing crime or serious impropriety
    ii protecting public health and safety
    iii preventing the public from being misled by an action or statement of an individual or organisation.

2 There is a public interest in freedom of expression itself.

3 Whenever the public interest is invoked, the PCC will require editors to demonstrate fully how the public interest was served.

4 The PCC will consider the extent to which material is already in the public domain or will become so.

5 In cases involving children under 16, editors must demonstrate an exceptional public interest to override the normally paramount interest of the child.

UNDER PRESSURE AND UNDER COVER

Investigative journalism plays a crucial role in a free press. Journalists spend weeks researching a story, going undercover and putting their own lives on hold and in danger to help expose and shame wrongdoers and, in many cases, get them put behind bars. How far, though, can journalists go in their investigations?

The Editor's Code of Practice allows for the use of subterfuge, provided it is in the public interest and that the story cannot be obtained by any other means. It means that newspapers must not undertake 'fishing expeditions', but they can use subterfuge in situations where they are dealing with wrongdoers who might seek to suppress evidence were they to be questioned in a more traditional way.

However, this ruling does not give automatic and cast-iron protection. *Evening Standard* reporter Wayne Veysey became the first journalist to face court charges of dishonesty and forgery in May 2003 after going undercover a year earlier to try and obtain a job as a cleaner at Heathrow Airport in order to write a story about security levels.

The judge in his case took the view that it was in the public interest that a poor standard of safety and security should always be liable to exposure in the free press and that some subterfuge had been acceptable. Veysey walked free from court after the charges against him had been dropped.

However, the judge's ruling does not give carte blanche to trainee journalists who believe that the only way to get a condition check on a hospital patient is to dress up as a doctor and sneak on to the wards (see Code of Practice above).

PERCEPTIONS OF THE PRESS

Watch how reporters are portrayed on any TV soap and you will see a braying pack of hounds climbing over picket fences, banging on doors, shouting and waving chequebooks. They might as well be wearing trench coats and trilby hats complete with 'Press' stickers, so rooted are these stereotypical images in television producers' minds. Sure, there are those journalists who operate using the gung-ho, come-on-luv-tell-us-all-about-it, tabloid style for extracting information from people, but we would argue that the majority of reporters go about their business in a much more civilised and respectable way – particularly those working on local and regional newspapers, where their role in the local community is something more than that of a smash-and-grab merchant.

Mike Hill, assistant editor of the *Lancashire Evening Post*, says that a common perception of a journalist is that featured in episodes of the television police series *The Bill* and its ilk, where journalists can be found rooting around in dustbins:

> People have a stereotypical image of journalists – like they do of politicians, lawyers and estate agents – and they will have that image until they meet the real thing. My reporters are not encouraged to behave like tabloid reporters and I don't think many local or regional reporters are.

Chris Page, editor of the *Selby Times*, says that there is a perception that journalists are only interested in using people to get stories: 'But it's more complicated than that.' Yes, he admits, his role as a journalist requires him to report on the things that are going on in his town and sometimes that means offending and upsetting people. At the same time, he sees himself as being as much a part of the local community as the people he writes about and that means taking a responsible, sometimes pragmatic, approach. In short, there are times when it is better to respect a source's desire for privacy than risk destroying a valuable and mutually beneficial relationship. On the other hand, Page often finds that a softly-softly approach, built on the trust and respect he has established over long years in the job, often yields dividends anyway. For instance, in early 2004, he secured an exclusive interview with the former wife of a suspect who went on the run after a murder in Leeds. She was willing to speak because she knew and trusted him. 'We can't be gung-ho about it,' says Page. 'We're dealing with people on a daily basis and if we upset them unnecessarily they're not going to deal with us again.'

> Paul Stimpson, deputy sports editor of the *Cambridge Evening News*, believes that all journalists tend to be tarred with the same brush – that of chequebook-waving hacks feasting on human misery and sensationalism: 'I once had a door shut in my face, when working on a fairly innocuous local story, with the words, "Your sort killed Diana".' However, he thinks that people tend to be better disposed towards sports journalists than news journalists: 'Perhaps sport is perceived as more glamorous or less sleazy.'

David Todd, assistant editor of the *Sheffield Star*, agrees that newspapers have to be sensitive to the needs of their communities:

> The only way to succeed is if people see it as their paper. We are here to inform people and help them – even if that means printing what time the swimming baths are open.
>
> If you have an exciting story, that's great, but if it's an informative story about the community, that's great, too. The one thing that local newspapers can do that

nobody else can is cover their area. You can get instant news from other media – radio, television and the Internet – but the broadcast media doesn't have the local knowledge or the resources on the ground that we have.

HOW DO JOURNALISTS SEE THEMSELVES?

Too often, trainee journalists see the media as a place in which they can shine. One colleague taught a student who believed that, at the end of his postgraduate journalism course, he would be dropped by helicopter into war zones from where he would report for BBC TV, Radio 4 and *The Guardian*. Nice work if you can get it, but hardly a realistic supposition. There are trainees at the other end of the scale who are not quite as energetic, believing that working on a newspaper will be a doddle. Sure, they want to right wrongs, but they don't want to have to work too hard getting facts and checking details. When asked if the spelling of their interviewee's name is correct, they say 'I think so'; when asked for an age, they reply that they 'didn't like to ask'.

Mike Hill believes that there is a general lack of hunger among new young reporters and he blames the plethora of courses offering 'media studies' that churn more young people into the market as 'journalists', but who are not journalists as traditionalists understand the term: 'They are missing the hunger to tell people what is going on and to get their stories on the front page. There is no hunger for the killer quote; the killer fact. I think reporting has become a nine-to-five job for some of them.' It is a shame because if you leave the newsroom to go home on the dot at 5 pm and a story breaks at 5.05 pm, you have missed it.

However, Hill believes that young reporters are 'cleaner' than some of their older, more experienced, and perhaps cynical, colleagues:

I sometimes have to tell them to be devious or cunning. When someone is being deliberately obstructive for no good reason other than trying to cover up wrongdoing, I don't think there is anything wrong in trying to trick or push them. For instance, I would put a reporter undercover for a story on illegal immigrants being used for slave labour, but I wouldn't if it was a case of getting into a hospital where a *Coronation Street* star was being treated.

Journalists should see themselves as people who speak up for their readers, reporting issues that are important to them and campaigning on their behalf – we are very big on championing on behalf of those people who don't have a voice.

I have to remember that I am not only a journalist – I am a man in the pub as well, so I take the populist approach; I reflect the way society is and thinks.

Many weekly newspapers succeed because they see themselves as doing a service to the community. At the *Pontefract and Castleford Express*, editor David Ward says that his newspaper is almost totally parochial:

It's bread and butter stories that people want. For instance, we run four columns of planning applications – people want to know about Mrs Smith's plans for a conservatory. Same with court reporting – people want to know that Mr Jones down the road has been done for drink driving.

We are not looking for a local angle on a national story, unless there's an obvious one. For example, we had a scoop after September 11th because the brother of our news editor works in New York. He was late for work that morning and about three blocks away when it happened – so our story was about the former Castleford lad who escaped death.

We're a weekly paper so, apart from stories like that, we're not going to be able to tell readers about major events that they don't already know about because they'll have read all about it in the nationals.

Some journalists see themselves as being removed from their readers – particularly those who have a complaint. Newspapers take great pride in either *not* printing corrections and apologies or hiding them deep within their pages. However, Mike Hill says that, if it is appropriate, what is wrong with telling someone you are sorry they have been upset? 'It's not admitting guilt or liability. However, if someone attacks you because of something you have printed that you know is fair and accurate, you deal with it politely, but you defend your corner.'

Exercise

You are a trainee reporter covering court for the *Leodis Leader* when your former A-level English tutor appears before the court charged with possessing a small amount of amphetamines and ecstasy tablets. It is clear from the details of the case that the drugs were for his personal use and that there was no intention to supply others.

Afterwards, your former teacher approaches you and asks you, as a favour, not to file a report, because, if the case becomes public, he will face disciplinary action at school and could lose his job as a result.

As a student, you had a good personal relationship with this teacher – in fact, it is as a result of his extra coaching that you achieved the A-level English pass that you needed to get your dream job in journalism.

What do you do?

(Answers are given at the end of the book.)

ANSWERS TO THE EXERCISES

1 OPENING THE NEWSROOM DOOR

Essential qualities for a good journalist include being:

- a good listener
- a good, clear writer
- able to identify a news story
- able to work under pressure
- accurate
- articulate
- confident
- determined
- diplomatic
- energetic
- flexible
- grammatical
- honest
- motivated
- observant
- organised
- patient
- punctual
- tenacious
- unafraid of hard work

with:

- a nose for news
- good research and fact-gathering skills
- people skills
- time management.

2   WHAT IS NEWS?

The stories should be ranked in the following order, starting with the story
with the greatest news value for a large circulation evening newspaper in
Yorkshire.

- 11 – of most interest because it is likely to affect a lot of people within
  an important part of the circulation area.
- 4 – similarly, whichever way the vote goes, it is going to affect a large
  number of people, plus, it is a strong talking point for the county.
- 10 – football, finance and a bargain to boot at Leeds United – the story
  is a winner for readers of an evening paper based in Yorkshire.
- 2 – important because it affects a large number of people in the southern
  part of the region. Obviously, if the evening paper were based in
  Sheffield, this would be a top story.
- 5 – classic example of a C-list celebrity story but one an evening paper
  would follow because of its popular appeal.
- 9 – cancer scare stories abound, but this one is slightly more unusual
  and, if it were run in the summer months, it would be a concern to
  readers planning to be out in their gardens.
- 8 – international news is important to regional evenings. Obviously if
  one of those killed were from the region, it would be a top story.
- 3 – an unusual would-you-believe-it type of story, but of little other
  interest to readers in Yorkshire as the action is based well outside the
  region.
- 7 – mildly interesting because it's royalty, but as HRH spends a large
  part of his time on events like this and this one is outside the region,
  what is new, exciting or different about it? Obviously, if he were opening an art gallery in Leeds, Sheffield or York, for instance, it would be
  a good picture story for the regional evening.
- 12 – of little interest because, at this stage, it is just an announcement
  and there is nothing to see – and we don't know whose statue this is.
- 1 – clearly a try-on by the MP with little chance of success. The only
  interest might be if the MP was local.
- 6 – of little interest to readers in Yorkshire as (a) it happened well outside the circulation area and (b) no one was killed or seriously injured.

3   WRITING NEWS

Gulf war veteran turned bus driver Ted Jones ended up in hospital after
taking a wrong turn and crashing into the side of a house.

Ted, 48, was treated for minor injuries after the empty bus skidded on black ice and crashed into a house in Balmoral Road, Leodis.

Householder Joan Smith escaped unhurt but her kitchen was in ruins.

'I went through the whole of the first Gulf war without a scratch,' said Ted. 'But the first time I take a bus out I end up in hospital' (89 words).

5 SPECIALIST AREAS - COURT

1 a
2 c
3 b
4 b
5 a
6 c
7 c
8 a
9 a
10 b

Latin terms:

11 c
12 b
13 a

6 SPECIALIST AREAS - COUNCIL

This is a particularly newsy agenda – there are several items that might make preview pieces or follow-ups after the meeting.

1 Declarations of interest – possible story if a councillor or planning official declares a personal interest in any of the items on the agenda.
2 Conservation advisory group – minutes of the meeting, which are attached to the main agenda, may throw up possible items of interest.
3 Petitions – how have the councillors responded to petitions presented at the last meeting? Why? Recap on the reasons for those petitions. Reactions of petitioners? New road safety petition – who is presenting it? What measures do they want? Why?

4 Site visits – which sites have been visited (and will be visited) and why? What decisions have been taken about applications that required a visit by councillors and planning officials? Why?

5 Road closures – why do these roads need to be closed? How long will they remain closed? Which parts of the roads are affected? Will diversions be necessary? Will motorists/pedestrians face delays as a result? What do local residents/shoppers/motorists think about the closures?

6 Appeals – what are the results of the appeals? Why were these decisions taken? Who is affected? Why were the applications made? Reactions of the people/companies making the appeal? Reactions of people living nearby?

9 SOURCES AND CONTACTS BOOKS

1 The local hoteliers association, some of the hotels themselves, Tourist Information Office, Trading Standards.

2 The author, Tourist Information Office, a local historian, the local council, local leisure centres, clubs and organisations, local restaurants, local celebrities who still live in the town.

3 Local dog breeders (especially those breeding Yorkshire Terriers), a local vet, RSPCA, National Canine Defence League, the Kennel Club (organisers of Crufts).

4 EU PRO, local MEP, one of the large chocolate manufacturers, a food technologist (from the local university), The Chocolate Society, local retailers – either a sweetshop or supermarket.

10 INTERVIEWING

1 a Before you set off.

- Ask yourself the purpose of the interview – why is it taking place? What line does your news editor want the resulting story to take and how long does he or she want it to be?
- How much information is already available about the interviewee and the subject matter? Do as much background research as you can.
- Prepare a list of possible questions.
- Make sure that the time and place are convenient for you and you know how to reach your destination. Set off on time.
- Make sure that you are suitably dressed.

- Make sure that you have a notebook (with plenty of blank pages), pens and a pencil. If using a tape recorder, make sure that you know how it works and you have spare batteries.

b   During the interview.

- Refer back to your list of questions as often as necessary, but make sure that you listen to the answers and ask follow-up questions as necessary. Listen out for unexpected information. Remember, the aim of an interview is to get the interviewee talking, so do not dominate the conversation.
- Ask open-ended questions – who, what, why, where, when and how? Give the interviewee time to respond before moving on to the next question and do not ask multiple questions.
- Encourage the interviewee by smiling and nodding – it shows that you are interested, but be careful not to overdo it.
- As you take notes, leave a margin so that you can highlight any particularly interesting facts.
- Be polite and friendly.
- Ask a bucket question at the end – is there anything else you would like to tell me?
- Double-check spellings of names and places, ages, titles, marital status.

2   You would interview the following people.

- The police's public relations officer and would want to know the answers to the questions below.

  Have they identified the youth and made an arrest? (Essential because, if the youth has been arrested and charged, reporting restrictions will apply.) If not, what steps have they taken to arrest the youth? What steps do they intend to take? Why were they unable to attend the incident? (Officers might have been attending another more serious incident.) Has this happened before? (When? Where? What happened then?) How many officers were on duty at the time? How many officers should have been on duty? Why were they so short of officers? (Might be a recruitment crisis – if so, why? Perhaps, instead, half the force is on sick leave – if so, why?)
- Staff at the store and would want to know the answers to the questions below.

  When did the incident take place? What made them suspicious about the alleged shoplifter? What was he doing? What did they do? What happened next? How did they restrain him? What did they think when police told them to parade him before the store's CCTV camera? Did they do it? What does the youth look like? What was he wearing? Was he alone? How did he react to being detained? How did he react to being paraded in front of the CCTV camera? And also to being released? How did they feel when they had to let him go? Is shoplifting a big problem?

Remember, depending on the responses to these questions, it might be necessary to ask follow-up questions.

Because you are looking for only 250 words, you might get enough information from these two sources to meet your word count. However, you might also consider speaking to the chair of your local police committee, a Police Federation representative and a spokesperson for the local Chamber of Trade.

11 ONLINE JOURNALISM

Council planning story, rewritten for the Web.

> More than 300 people have signed a petition objecting to the extension of a sauna and massage parlour in Balmoral Road, Leodis.
>
> The proprietor of The Pampas Rooms wants to expand into adjoining premises but nearby residents claim that the expansion is inappropriate in a residential area.
>
> However, officials advising members of the Leodis city centre and south planning subcommittee say that there are no legitimate planning grounds for refusing the application and the concerns of residents cannot be taken into consideration.

Links might be provided to:

- The website of the Leodis city centre and south planning subcommittee where full details of the application are displayed, together with the recommendations of planning officials.
- An information piece explaining the functions and responsibilities of the subcommittee.
- Composite profiles of the members of the committee.
- A table showing how many applications are considered by the committee each month, how many are refused and the reasons.
- An exclusive interview with residents outlining their objections.
- Composite profiles of the key members of the residents' campaign.
- An information piece explaining the grounds on which planning applications may be refused.

- The Pampas Rooms' website.
- A map showing the location of The Pampas Rooms.
- A profile of the proprietor, discussing his plans for the business.

12 THE JOURNALIST IN SOCIETY

Although possession of amphetamines and ecstasy tablets is a criminal offence, you do not consider it a serious crime. However, society as a whole does not share your view on this matter. Your mother, for instance, would be very concerned about the teacher's consumption of illegal drugs. Mum would worry that his lax views on drugtaking might be passed on to the children he is teaching.

The point here is that your personal views about soft drugs are irrelevant – your decisions have to be based on what best serves the wider interests of the community as a whole. In this case, your readers deserve to be informed that a person who occupies a position of moral and social responsibility with regard to local youngsters has an illegal drugs habit. Many of those readers may consider that this does not make him a better or worse teacher, but, as the matter is serious enough to warrant a court appearance and a substantial fine, they should be given the facts so that they can make up their own minds. Further, the teacher, in choosing to consume substances that he knows to be illegal, must, as a mature adult, accept the consequences of his actions.

As a journalist, your job is to inform your news editor about what has happened and write a full and accurate report of the proceedings.

GLOSSARY OF TERMS

ABC   Audit Bureau of Circulation, which produces newspaper circulation figures.

Advertorial   text that looks like editorial, but is paid for by the advertiser.

Angle   the particular line or point taken or made by a reporter in a story.

Backgrounder   an explanatory feature (often shorter than other features) that adds information and/or colour to a news story.

Back issue   a previous issue of a newspaper.

Banner headline   large, front-page headline.

Billboard   an advertising board (often found outside newspaper offices and newsagents) summarising a particular story.

Box   text enclosed in a box on the page. Often used for extra facts or to highlight a particular piece of text.

Broadsheets   traditionally large-format, quality newspapers, such as *The Daily Telegraph* and *The Guardian* – sometimes also called heavies. *See also* Tabloids.

Byline   name of journalist displayed with the story that he or she has written.

Calls   telephone checks to emergency services for incident details and updates.

Campaign   newspapers often run campaigns of their own to promote a particular issue or a single reporter could gain a reputation as a campaigning journalist.

Caption   a line of descriptive text accompanying a photograph.

Catchline   a one-word title given by the reporter to a story.

Centre spread   a story or feature that runs across two pages in the centre of the newspaper.

Colour   descriptive detail added to a story.

Columnist   a journalist who produces his or her own column or opinion piece.

Conference   a meeting between the editor and/or departmental heads to discuss that day's newspaper's content.

Contacts   a journalist's sources for stories and information.

Copy   the text before it is typeset. Hard copy is that printed on paper.

Corr   correspondent or specialist, as in health corr, education corr.

Crop   to reduce a picture.

Crosshead   a small, one- or two-word heading used to break up a column of type on a page.

Cut   remove text from a story or a story from the page.

Cuttings   extracts taken from newspapers and filed under subject headings (usually kept in the newspaper's library).

Deadline   the time to which all journalists must work, be it to submit copy, have pages prepared for printing or have the newspaper out on the streets.

Death knock   where a reporter goes to the home of someone who has died to interview relatives and friends and collect a picture of the deceased, such as a school photo of a young boy killed in a road accident.

Deck   a single line in a headline.

Delayed drop   a type of intro that delays giving certain facts to add impact.

Diary   the office 'bible' that lists jobs that must be covered on a particular day.

Dig   the description given to the research process that a journalist must undertake while working on stories.

Doorknocking   literally that – knocking on doors in the hope of finding witnesses to and/or commentators on incidents and events that have happened locally.

Doorstepping   a more persistent form of doorknocking, whereby the reporter waits or 'camps' outside the home of a particular source. Often occurs in relation to celebrities, shamed MPs or shady businesspeople.

Double-page spread   a story or feature that covers two pages.

Editorial   any text that is not advertising, but, also, a leading article that expresses the newspaper's opinion, as in a 'leader'.

Embargo   a date and, sometimes, time before which information should not be published. Usually imposed by an organisation sending information via a press release.

Exclusive   a story supposedly unique to the newspaper making the claim, but very much over-used nowadays. Beware the type of newspaper that declares a story, lifted from a smaller weekly or evening newspaper, is its own exclusive.

Eyewitness   either an interviewee who has seen a particular incident or event taking place or the reporter him- or herself who is writing an eyewitness account.

Fact box   added information, facts, figures or statistics usually published as a box or side bar to the main story.

Feature   an article that is longer than a news story, goes into more detail and usually contains more information, colour, humour and quotes.

File   the way in which reporters send in their stories.

Filler   a short story of one or two pars to literally fill space.

Follow-up   an update on an earlier story.

Free   a newspaper that is distributed or given away free. Often weeklies.

Freebies   free products, services or trips supplied to journalists. Also known as perks.

Freelance a journalist (often self-employed) who writes for more than one publication.

Heavies *see* Broadsheets.

House style the spelling and other preferences and grammatical rules followed by a particular publication.

In-house something peculiar to a particular organisation, such as an organisation's own 'in-house' or internal communications newsletter.

Intro the first sentence or par of a story.

Inverted triangle a classic way of constructing a story. Also known as an inverted pyramid structure.

Kill an instruction to cancel a story or page.

Layout the way in which stories, pictures and ads are designed and presented on the page.

Leader *see* Editorial.

Legal to check (usually through the newspaper's lawyer) that a story does not commit libel or contempt or contravene any other laws.

Linage payment based on the number of lines in a story.

Lower case small letters used rather than capitals.

Masthead the title of the newspaper found on the front page.

NIB news in brief. Short, one- or two-par stories, often found in a column of NIBs down one side of the page.

Obit short for obituary.

Off-diary a story that has not been listed in the newsroom diary – in other words, a story that a reporter has found using his or her own resources.

Off-the-record information or briefings that should not be credited or traceable to the source.

Opinion piece a personal column expressing the views of the writer.

Par or para short for paragraph.

Peg   the reason for writing the story.

Perks   *see* Freebies.

Pick up   often used in reference to pictures, as in, collecting a picture of a victim from his or her home or literally picking up a picture that has been supplied at a press conference or meeting.

Piece   often used to describe a story or feature.

Pix   short for pictures.

Press release   information sent to the media by an organisation to make an announcement or promote a particular event or service. Often written by the press relations officer representing the particular organisation.

PRO   press relations officer.

Pyramid   *see* Inverted triangle.

Quotes   the things interviewees say. Displayed in the story in quote marks (short for quotation marks).

Red tops   traditionally these were tabloid newspapers, such as *The Sun, The Mirror* and *Daily Sport. See also* Broadsheets *and* Tabloids.

Rejig   rewrite or rework copy – something a news editor or sub will tell a reporter to do when their original copy does not tell the story as well as it could.

Running story   a story that runs for several days as new information is added (often used in stories involving murder hunts and missing children where regular updates are being given each day by police).

Scoop   an exclusive story.

Screamer   an exclamation mark.

Sidebar   a side panel in which extra information can be displayed.

Spike   a story that has been rejected is spiked. This comes from the fact that, some years ago, a metal spike was used to pierce and hold dead copy.

Splash   front page lead story.

Spoiler a story put out by one publication to lessen the impact of a rival's story.

Standfirst lines of text under the headline of a story that offer added information and often include the reporter's byline.

Story the account of an incident or event written by the reporter.

Stringer a freelancer who contributes regularly to a particular publication.

Sub the sub-editor who edits a reporter's copy, writes headlines and designs the layout of pages.

Tabloids newspapers that are about half the size of the broadsheets. The national popular press, 'red tops' and many regional evening newspapers are tabloid, and the former broadsheets, the *Independent* and *The Times*, are also now available in the handier compact size. *See also* Red tops *and* Broadsheets.

Think piece a personal opinion column that discusses a particular issue.

Tip-off information from a source or member of the public.

Upper case capital letter.

Vox pop a series of quotes from a variety of people on a particular theme or issue usually accompanied by photographs. Means the 'voice of the people'.

BIBLIOGRAPHY

Alcott, Louisa M. (1983, reprint) *Good Wives*. London: Penguin.

Bagnall, Nicholas (1993) *Newspaper Language*. Oxford: Focal Press.

Barber, Lynn (2000) 'The art of the interview', in Stephen Glover (ed.) *The Penguin Book of Journalism: Secrets of the press*. London: Penguin.

Barnabas, Ben (2003) 'Rageh Omaar wins it for BBC in Baghdad', *The Guardian*, 14 April.

Bell, A. (1991) *The Language of News Media*. Oxford: Blackwell.

Blood, Rebecca (2000) *Weblogs: A history and perspective*. www.rebeccablood.net/essays/weblog_history.html

Blood, Rebecca (2002) *The Weblog Handbook: Practical advice on creating and maintaining your blog*. Philadelphia, Pennsylvania: Perseus.

Bocking, David (2004) 'Scouts riding the wave', *Sheffield Telegraph*, 20 February.

Bolt, Robert (2001) *A Man for All Seasons*. London: Methuen.

Bonime, Andrew, and Pohlmann, Ken (1998) *Writing for New Media: The essential guide to writing for interactive media, CD-ROMS and the Web*. New York: J. Wiley.

Byrne, Ciar (2003) 'Reporting truth about war proving difficult, says BBC news chief', *The Guardian*, 26 March.

Clayton, Joan (1992) *Journalism for Beginners: How to get into print and get paid for it*. London: Piakus.

Coetzee, J. M. (1986) *Foe*. London: Penguin.

Cram, Ian (1998) 'Sex and violence in fact and fiction', in Matthew Kieran (ed.) *Media Ethics*. London: Routledge.

Crompton, Richmal (1992) *William and the Space Animal*. London and Basingstoke: Macmillan Children's Books.

Crystal, David (1995) *The Cambridge Encyclopedia of the English Language*. Cambridge: Cambridge University Press.

Dahlgren, P., and Sparks, C. (eds) (2000) *Journalism and Popular Culture*. London: Sage.

D'Arcy, Mark (2001, reprint) 'Local power and public accountability: an example from the East Midlands', in Hugo de Burgh (ed.) *Investigative Journalism: Context and practice*. London: Routledge.

Daily Mail (2001) 'Goran agrees to lead the British tennis revolution', 11 July.

Daily Mail (2002) 'Who cares? At 108, Alice Knight starved herself to death, a despairing victim of how our old people's homes have been wrecked by red tape and cost cutting', 3 July.

The Daily Telegraph (2002) 'Tear up chaotic planning reforms, say MPs', 3 July.

de Burgh, H. (ed.) (2001, reprint) *Investigative Journalism: Context and practice*. London: Routledge.

Eastern Daily Press (2004) 'Rivals clashed at party', 12 March.

Ericson, R. V., Baranek, P. M., and Chan, J. B. L. (1999) 'Negotiating control: a study of news sources', in Howard Tumber (ed.) *News: A reader*. Oxford: Oxford University Press.

The Express (2004) 'Gene and tonic: science proves that alcoholics can't help it', 15 January.

Foot, Paul (2000) 'The slow death of investigative journalism', in Stephen Glover (ed.) *The Penguin Book of Journalism: Secrets of the press*. London: Penguin.

Fowler, Roger (1991) *Language in the News: Discourse and ideology in the press*. London: Routledge.

Frayn, Michael (2003) *The Tin Men*. London: Faber & Faber.

Gieber, Walter (1999) 'News is what newspapermen make it', in Howard Tumber (ed.) *News: A reader*. Oxford: Oxford University Press.

Glover, Stephen (ed.) (2000) *The Penguin Book of Journalism: Secrets of the press*. London: Penguin.

The Guardian (1999) 'He's been arrested 80 times, he's blamed for 1,000 offences. Can anyone save him?', 25 March.

The Guardian (2003) 'Further hitch in Regan trial', 22 January.

The Guardian (2003) 'Dismay at chemical plant link', 7 March.

The Guardian (2003) 'Tooth fairy posts 100% dividend', 7 March.

The Guardian (2003) 'Free to do bad things', 12 April.

The Guardian (2003) 'Rageh Omaar wins it for BBC in Baghdad', 14 April.

The Guardian (2004) 'Scots lament the Hogmanay that never was', 2 January.

The Guardian (2004) 'The final betrayal', 14 January.

Hall, Debbie (2004) 'No kidding ... these goats are BIG cheeses', *The Journal*, January.

Harcup, Tony (2004) *Journalism: Principles and practice*. London: Sage.

Harcup, Tony, and O'Neill, Deirdre (2001) 'What is news? Galtung and Ruge revisited', *Journalism Studies*, 2(2) May. London: Routledge.

Hargreaves, Ian (2003) *Journalism: Truth or dare?* Oxford: Oxford University Press.

Harris, Geoffrey, and Spark, David (1998, reprint) *Practical Newspaper Reporting*. Oxford: Focal Press.

Herman, E. S., and Chomsky, N. (1999) 'Manufacturing content', in Howard Tumber (ed.) *News: A reader*. Oxford: Oxford University Press.

Hicks, Wynford (1999, reprint) *English for Journalists*. London: Routledge.

Hicks, Wynford, Adams, Sally, and Gilbert, Harriett (1999) *Writing for Journalists*. London: Routledge.

Holtby, Winifred (1981) *South Riding*. Glasgow: Fontana/Collins.

Keeble, Richard (1998) *The Newspapers Handbook*. London: Routledge.

Lacey, C., and Longman, D. (1997) *The Press as Public Educator: Cultures of understanding, cultures of ignorance*. Luton: University of Luton.

Lancashire Evening Post (2003) 'The birth of baby Jesus ... and no school for ages', 18 December.

Langer, John (2000, reprint) 'Truly awful news on television', in P. Dahlgren and C. Sparks (eds) *Journalism and Popular Culture*. London: Sage.

Lewycka, Marina, Senior Lecturer in Professional Writing, Sheffield Hallam University, conversation, 12 March 2003.

Luke, Harding (2001) 'In half a minute everyone was killed', *The Guardian*, 20 January.

MacShane, Denis (1979) *Using the Media: How to deal with the press, television and radio*. London: Pluto Press.

McKain, B., Bonnington, A. J., McInnes, R., and Clive, E. M. (2000) *Scots Law for Journalists*. Edinburgh: W. Green.

McManus, J. H. (1999) 'Market driven journalism: let the citizen beware', in Howard Tumber (ed.) *News: A reader*. Oxford: Oxford University Press.

McNair, Brian (2001, reprint) *News and Journalism in the UK*. London: Routledge.

McQuail, Denis (1996) 'Mass media in the public interest', in J. Curran and M. Gurevitch (eds) *Mass and Society*. London: Arnold.

Masterman, Len (1994, reprint) *Teaching the Media*. London: Routledge.

Matheson, D. (2004) 'Weblogs and the epistemology of the news: some trends in online journalism', *New Media & Society*, 6 (4): 443–68.

Milne, A. A. (2000) *Winnie-the-Pooh*. London: Egmont.

The Mirror (2003) 'Adult violence link to kids' TV', 10 March.

The Mirror (2004) 'Aloud mouth; singer Nicola's drunken shame in club', 15 January.

The Mirror (2004) 'Ramsay cooks up TV show', 15 January.

The Mirror (2004) 'Splosh idol', 15 January.

Nottingham Evening Post (2004) 'City centre sex attack', 7 January.

Nottingham Evening Post (2004) 'No progress on bus pay', 7 January.

Nottingham Evening Post (2004) 'Woman fined for dog mess', 7 January.

Nottingham Evening Post (2004) 'Yob is banned from city area', 7 January.

The Observer (2003) 'BBC defends its reporter in Baghdad', 13 April.

Orwell, George (1984) 'Politics and the English language', in *The Penguin Essays of George Orwell*. London: Penguin.

Press Gazette (2003) 'Tips of trade: theatre reviewers', 7 March.

Preston, Peter (2003) 'Here is the news: too much heat ... too little light', *The Observer*, 30 March.

Radford, Tim (2004) 'Experts have their cake and eat it', *The Guardian*, 14 January.

Randall, David (2000) *The Universal Journalist*. London: Pluto Press.

Reah, Danuta (1998) *The Language of Newspapers*. London: Routledge.

Reeves, Ian (2002) 'Jean's PG tips', *Press Gazette*, 11 January.

Rocco, Fiammetta (2000) 'Journalists taken hostage', in Stephen Glover (ed.) *The Penguin Book of Journalism: Secrets of the press*. London: Penguin.

Rowe, David (2000) 'Modes of sport', in P. Dahlgren and C. Sparks (eds) *Journalism and Popular Culture*. London: Sage.

Sheffield Telegraph (2004) 'It's a question of trust – who will the rank and file back?', 20 February.

Sheffield Telegraph (2004) 'Scouts riding the wave', 20 February.

Sheffield Telegraph (2004) 'Wednesday's future secure, says Allen', 20 February.

Sheridan Burns, Lynette (2000) *Understanding Journalism*. London: Sage.

Silverstone, R. (1999) *Why Study the Media?* London: Sage.

Stephenson, David (1998) *How to Succeed in Newspaper Journalism*. London: Kogan Page.

The Sun (2001) 'Blunkett: I'll crush riots', 9 July.

The Sun (2002) 'Never a rape: snooker case insult to real victims', 3 July.

Thorpe, Vanessa (2003) 'BBC defends its reporter in Baghdad', *The Observer*, 13 April.

Truss, Lynne (2003) *Eats, Shoots and Leaves: The zero tolerance approach to punctuation*. London: Profile.

Tumber, Howard (1999) *News: A reader*. Oxford: Oxford University Press.

Wakefield Express (2004) 'Killer's body was burned', 16 January.

Ward, Mike (2002) *Journalism Online*. Oxford: Focal Press.

Waterhouse, Keith (1978) *Billy Liar*. London: Penguin.

Waugh, Evelyn (1982) *Scoop*. London: Penguin.

Welsh, T., and Greenwood, W. (eds) (2003, reprint) *McNae's Essential Law for Journalists*. London: Butterworths.

Wheen, F. (2002) *Hoo-Hahs and Passing Frenzies: Collected journalism 1991–2001.* London: Atlantic Books.

Whitaker, Brian (2003) 'Free to do bad things', *The Guardian*, 12 April.

White, Lesley (2001) 'Puff Daddy', *The Sunday Times Magazine*, 4 February.

Wilde, J. (2003) 'Plain English', lecture at Sheffield Hallam University, 17 October.

Williams, K. (1977) *The English Newspaper.* London: Springwood Books.

Williams, Richard (2004) 'India and Pakistan break the ice and conjure "something unique"', *The Guardian*, 15 March.

Wodehouse, P. G. (1975) *Bachelors Anonymous.* London: Penguin.

Worsthorne, Peregrine (2000) 'Dumbing up', in S. Glover (ed.) *The Penguin Book of Journalism: Secrets of the press.* London: Penguin.

www.hmcourts-service.gov.uk

Yorkshire Evening Post (1999) 'Can bombs defuse a powder keg?', 25 March.

Yorkshire Evening Post (2004) 'More strings to his bow', 6 January.

INDEX